# PRELUDE:
# What If ?

What if life were perfect?

What if you lived in a perfect world of perfect people and perfect possessions, with everyone and everything doing the perfect thing at the perfect time?

What if you had everything you wanted, and only what you wanted, exactly as you wanted, precisely when you wanted it?

What if, after luxuriating in this perfect world for the perfect length of time, you started feeling uneasy about the predictability of perfection?

What if, after an additional perfect length of time, you began thinking, "There seems to be a lack of risk, adventure, and fun in perfection. 'Having it my way' all the time is getting dull."

What if, after yet another perfect length of time, you decided, "Perfection is a perfect bore."

What if, at that point in your perfect world, you created a button marked, "Surprise."

What if you walked over, considered all that might be contained in the concept of "surprise," decided, "Anything's better than boredom," took a deep breath, pushed the button . . .

i

. . . and found yourself where you are right now—feeling what you're feeling now, thinking what you're thinking now, with everything in your life precisely the way it is now—reading this book.

*The essence of our effort to see
that every child has a chance
must be to assure
each an equal opportunity,
not to become equal,
but to become different—
to realize whatever unique
potential of body,
mind and spirit
he or she possesses.*

JOHN FISCHER

# LIFE 101

**Everything We Wish We
Had Learned About Life
In School—But Didn't**

# Peter McWilliams

Prelude Press
8159 Santa Monica Boulevard
Los Angeles, California 90046

**1-800-LIFE-101**

ISBN: 0-931580-64-1

Editor: Jean Sedillos
Desktop publishing: Carol Taylor
Production: Paurvi Trivedi
Research: Michael D. Hartl

*At college age,*
*you can tell who is best*
*at taking tests and going to school,*
*but you can't tell*
*who the best people are.*
*That worries the hell*
*out of me.*

BARNABY C. KEENEY

# Contents

# PART TWO
## ADVANCED TOOLS FOR EAGER

# PART THREE
## MASTER TEACHERS IN DISGUISE .. 185

# PART FOUR
## TOOLS FOR SUCCESFUL DOERS ..... 267

# PART FIVE
## TO HAVE JOY AND TO HAVE IT MORE ABUNDANTLY

# APPENDIX
## SELECTIONS FROM OTHER BOOKS
### BY PETER McWILLIAMS

*The other line*
*always moves faster.*

BARBARA ETTORE

# LIFE 101

**Everything We Wish We
Had Learned About Life
In School—But Didn't**

*Only the curious will learn
and only the resolute
overcome the obstacles
to learning.
The quest quotient has
always excited me more
than the intelligence quotient.*

EUGENE S. WILSON

# PART ONE

## INTRODUCTION TO LIFE

Welcome to life.

I call this book *LIFE 101* because it contains all the things I wish I had learned about life in school but, for the most part, did not.

After twelve (or more) years of schooling, we know how to figure the square root of an isosceles triangle (invaluable in daily life), but we might not know how to forgive ourselves and others.

We know what direction migrating birds fly in autumn, but we're not sure which way we want to go.

We have dissected a frog, but perhaps have never explored the dynamics of human relationships.

We know who wrote "To be or not to be, that is the question," but we don't know the answer.

We know what pi is, but we're not sure who we are.

We may know how to diagram a sentence, but we may not know how to love ourselves.

That our educational system is not designed to teach us the "secrets of life" is no secret. In school, we learn how to do everything—except how to live.

> **Fred Sanford:** *Didn't you learn*
> *anything being my son?*
> *Who do you think I'm*
> *doing this all for?*
>
> **Lamont Sanford:** *Yourself.*
>
> **Fred:** *Yeah, you*
> *learned something.*

Maybe that's the way it should be. Unraveling life's "mysteries" and discovering life's "secrets" (which are, in fact, neither mysterious nor secretive) may take the courage and determination found only in a self-motivated pursuit.

You probably already know there's more to life than reading, 'riting, and 'rithmetic. I'm glad you learned reading, of course, or you wouldn't be able to read this book. I'm also glad I learned 'riting (such as it is).

And 'rithmetic? Well, as Mae West once said, "One and one is two, two and two are four, and five'll get you ten if you know how to work it." That's what this book is about: knowing how to work it, and having fun along the way.

Although a lot can be learned from adversity, most of the same lessons can be learned through enjoyment and laughter. If you're like me, you've probably had more than enough adversity. (After graduating from the School of Hard Knocks, I automatically enrolled in the University of Adversity.)

I agree with Alan Watts, who said, "I am *sincere* about life, but I'm not *serious* about it." If you're looking for serious, pedantic, didactic instruction, you will not find it here. I will—with a light heart— present hundreds of techniques and suggestions, and for each of them I make the same suggestion:

Give it a try.

If it works for you, fine—use it; it's yours. If it doesn't work for you, let it go and try other things that may. When you find things that *do* work for you, I advise you to follow Shakespeare's advice: "Grapple them to thy soul with hoops of steel."

Naturally, not everything in *LIFE 101* will be for you. I'm laying out a smorgasbord. The carrot-raisin salad you pass up may be the very thing another person craves, while the caviar you're making a beeline for might be just so much salty black stuff to the carrot-salad lover.

If I say something you find not "true," please don't discount everything else in the book. It may be "true" for someone else. That same someone else might say, "What nonsense," about something which has you knowingly muttering, "How true." It's a big world; we are all at different points on our

> *We don't receive wisdom;*
> *we must discover it*
> *for ourselves after a journey*
> *that no one can take for us*
> *or spare us.*
>
> MARCEL PROUST

personal journeys. Life has many truths; take what you can use and leave the rest.

If you take from this book ten percent—any ten percent—and use it as your own, I'll consider my job well done.

Which brings me to the question: Who is the *real* teacher of *LIFE 101?* I'll get to that shortly. (Hint: It's certainly not me—or *I,* as the grammatically correct among us would say.) (Second hint: It is *definitely* not me.)

For now, welcome to *LIFE 101*. When you were born, you probably had quite a welcome, although you may have been too young to remember it. So, as you begin this "life," please feel welcome.

Although it may be "just a book," it's a book of ideas from my mind to yours; a book of best wishes from my heart to yours. As James Burke observed, "When you read a book, you hold another's mind in your hands." (So be careful!) Here's to our time together being intimate, enjoyable, and loving.

Welcome.

*Life is far too important a thing
ever to talk about.*

Oscar Wilde

# Why Life?

What's it all about? Why are we here? What's the point? *Is* there a point? Why bother?

Why life?

At some point, you have probably pondered The Meaning of Life, and you came up with a satisfactory answer, which either has or has not stood the test of time, or you shrugged mightily, muttered, "Beats the hell out of me," and ordered another cheeseburger.*

The question which precedes "What's the meaning of life?" is, of course, "*Is there* a meaning to life?" Beats the hell out of me. I'm going to explore the first question *as though* the answer to the second question is yes.

If it's true that life has no meaning—no purpose—then it doesn't matter whether I've consumed a few pages speculating on the meaning of life. So let's play a game called "Life Matters."

We'll start the game by *assuming* there is a purpose. The first question of Life Matters: "What is the purpose of life?"

Here's my answer:

Life is for doing, learning, and enjoying.

---

*HOMEWORK: Watch a video of the Monty Python movie, *The Meaning of Life*. Very funny; very true.

*Things won are done;*
*joy's soul lies in the doing.*

SHAKESPEARE

# Doing

One thing about humans: we are *doing* creatures. When we're not doing something, we're *thinking* about doing something, which, in its own way, *is* doing something. When we sleep, we toss and dream. We exercise to keep our bodies in shape so we can do some more.

We are well designed for doing. Unlike trees, our bodies can move from place to place. In a matter of seconds, our emotions can move from happy to sad and back again. Our thoughts move us to places we can't go physically—our memory moves us back in time, our intelligence anticipates future movement, and our imagination takes us to places we've never been.

As to nature—you name it, and humans have either changed it, processed it, painted it, preserved it, moved it, or done *something* to it. (At the very least, we *named* it.) We seem bent on rearranging the world.

The theatrical director Moss Hart had a country home. He would visit on weekends, and request of his landscape designer that a few trees be put over there, a stream over here, and please move that mountain a few hundred feet to the left. When playwright George S. Kaufman visited Hart's home, he remarked, "This is the way God would do it if He only had money."

It's often been observed that, from afar, the doing of humans resembles the bustling of ants. We

> *The shortest answer is doing.*
>
> LORD HERBERT
>
> 1583–1648

must occasionally wonder, "What *is* the purpose of all this doing?" We are not, after all, rocks, which don't seem to do much at all. We have the ability to do, but why?

We must, of course, do in order to meet our bodily needs (which would not be as great if we did not do as much), but even after these needs are met, we keep on doing. Why?

My suggestion:

Our doing allows for more learning.

*Learning is not*
*attended by chance,*
*it must be sought for with ardor*
*and attended to with diligence.*

ABIGAIL ADAMS

1780

*Wear your learning,*
*like your watch,*
*in a private pocket:*
*and do not pull it out*
*and strike it,*
*merely to show*
*that you have one.*

EARL OF CHESTERFIELD

1774

# Learning

Life is for learning? Learning what? You name it. There's a lot to learn. In just the first five years of life we learned physical coordination, walking, talking, eating, going potty, interaction with family and playmates, a great many facts about this planet, and all the other things that differentiate a five-year-old from a newborn infant.

From age five to ten we learned reading, writing, arithmetic, geography, history, science, music, sports—and when we weren't watching television we learned some more about people: friends, relatives, enemies, allies, rivals, supporters, detractors.

Some of what we learned early on turned out to be true (the earth is round; if you want a friend, be a friend; cleanliness is next to impossible) and some of it turned out to be false (Santa Claus; the Tooth Fairy; Kansas is more fun than Oz).

Some things had to be relearned—or unlearned—and while relearning and unlearning, maybe we learned what to do about disappointment—and maybe we didn't.

Looking in on most lives, we see dramatic growth until the age of fifteen or twenty. Then the growing slows, stops, or, in some cases, regresses.

Most people declare themselves "done" when their formal education is complete. What is it about renting a cap and gown and receiving a scroll of paper that makes us think our learning days are over?

*I call that mind free which jealously guards its intellectual rights and powers, which calls no man master, which does not content itself with a passive or hereditary faith, which opens itself to light whencesoever it may come, which receives new truth as an angel from Heaven.*

WILLIAM ELLERY CHANNING

1829

It's not that there's nothing left to learn. Far from it. "Commencement" does not just mean graduation; it means a new beginning.

The more we learn, the more we do. The more we do, the more we learn. But in all this doing and learning, let's not forget one of the most important lessons of all—enjoyment.

*How good is man's life,*
*the mere living!*
*How fit to employ all the heart*
*and the soul and the senses*
*forever in joy!*

ROBERT BROWNING

1855

*Seek not, my soul,*
*the life of the immortals;*
*but enjoy to the full*
*the resources*
*that are within thy reach.*

PINDAR

518–438 B.C.

# Enjoying

*Joy* is an interesting word. It does not have an automatic opposite created by grafting "un" or "dis" or "in" onto it. There is pleasure and displeasure, happiness and unhappiness, gratitude and ingratitude—but there is no unjoy, disjoy, or injoy. (Can you imagine the word *in*enjoy?)

The old story comes to mind: Two brothers went to ride ponies on their uncle's ranch, but first the uncle insisted that they shovel a large pile of manure out of a stall. One brother hated the project, grumbling his way through a few halfhearted scoops. The other brother was laughing and singing and shoveling with abandon. "What are you so happy about?" the first brother asked. "Well," the second replied, "with all this manure, there must be a pony in here somewhere!"

So it is with life. When life seems truly excremental, we can moan and groan, or we can—even in the midst of anger, terror, confusion, and pain—tell ourselves, "There must be a lesson in here someplace!"

The trick, I think, is to learn to enjoy the process of learning. As Confucius observed 2,500 years ago, "With coarse rice to eat, with water to drink, and my bended arm for a pillow—I still have joy in the midst of these things."

"With an eye made quiet by the power of harmony, and the deep power of joy," wrote Wordsworth, "we see into the life of things."

*A man's life of any worth
is a continual allegory.*

JOHN KEATS

# Life Is a Metaphor

There are many models for life: analogies, allegories, and metaphors to help us understand something as complicated, intricate, and seemingly ununderstandable as life.

There is the Life-Is-a-Game school of thought (and its many subschools: Life Is a Baseball Game, Life Is a Football Game, Life Is Like Tennis, Life Is Chess, Life's Like Monopoly, Life As Croquet).

"Life is like a game of whist," Eugene Hare pointed out some time ago. "From unseen sources the cards are shuffled, and the hands are dealt." Josh Billings completed the thought: "Life consists not in holding good cards but in playing those you hold well."

Some believe Life Is an Intricate Machine (very popular in Germany). In Northern California they believe Life Is a Computer. Buckminster Fuller synthesized the two: "The earth is like a spaceship that didn't come with an operating manual."

Is life work or play? Karl Marx said, "Living is working," and Henry Ford, of all people, agreed: "Life is work." Disagreeing is Leon de Montenaeken, who said, "Life is but play," and Liza de Minnelli, who sang, "Life is a cabaret."

Seneca said, "Life is a play. It's not its length, but its performance that counts." What kind of play is it? Jean de La Bruyere suggested life's "a tragedy for those who feel, a comedy for those who think." Kirk Douglas called life "a B-picture script." (From

> *The very purpose*
> *of existence is to reconcile*
> *the glowing opinion*
> *we hold of ourselves*
> *with the appalling things*
> *that other people*
> *think about us.*
>
> QUENTIN CRISP

Seneca to Kirk Douglas in one paragraph. Not bad.)

Shakespeare, of course, called life "a poor player, that struts and frets his hour upon the stage..." and James Thurber continued: "It's a tale told in an idiom, full of unsoundness and fury, signifying nonism." George Bernard Shaw also took the Bard to task: "Life is no brief candle to me. It is sort of a splendid torch that I have got hold of for the moment."

There are those who like musical analogies. "Life is something like a trumpet," the great W. C. Handy pointed out, "If you don't put anything in, you won't get anything out." Samuel Butler said, "Life is playing a violin solo in public and learning the instrument as one goes on." Ella Wheeler Wilcox sang, "Our lives are songs: God writes the words / and we set them to music at pleasure; / and the song grows glad, or sweet or sad / as we choose to fashion the measure."

One of the nicest literary analogies comes from the Jewish Theological Seminary: "A life is a single letter in the alphabet. It can be meaningless. Or it can be part of a great meaning."

One of the greatest letters in the American alphabet, Helen Keller, proclaimed, "Life is either a daring adventure, or nothing." George Bernard Shaw agreed: "Life is a series of inspired follies. The difficulty is to find them to do. Never lose a chance: it doesn't come every day."

How about closing this chapter with the Life-Is-Food contingent?

"Life is an onion," Carl Sandburg wrote. "You peel it off one layer at a time, and sometimes you weep." "Life is like eating artichokes," T. A. Dorgan tells us. "You've got to go through so much to get so little." Or maybe it's more as Auntie Mame pointed out: "Life is a banquet, and some poor sons-of-bitches are starving."

Don Marquis called life "a scrambled egg." Make of that what you will—but then, we could say that about life itself, couldn't we?

And what do I think life is? What model do I use to describe our time together? Please turn the page.

*Universities should be safe havens*
*where ruthless*
*examination of realities*
*will not be distorted*
*by the aim to please*
*or inhibited*
*by the risk of displeasure.*

KINGMAN BREWSTER

# Life Is a Classroom

It should come as no surprise that, if I think life is for learning, I would view the process of life itself as a classroom. But it's not a dull, sit-in-neat-little-rows-and-listen-to-some-puffed-up-professor-drone-on-and-on classroom. Life is (as I'm sure you've noticed) *experiential*. In that sense, life's more of a workshop.

I like to think the workshop/classroom of life is perfectly arranged so that we learn what we need to learn, when we need to learn it, just the way we need to learn it.

The operative word in all that is *need*, not *want*.

We don't always learn what we *want* to learn. In tenth-grade biology there was only one animal's reproductive methods I was interested in studying, but I had to start with splitting of amoebas (yawn) and work my way up. The biology teacher had a lesson plan different from mine.

And so, it seems, does life.

Life's lessons come in all shapes and sizes. Sometimes what we need to know we learn in a formal way, such as taking a class or reading a book. Sometimes we learn by an informal, seemingly accidental process: an overheard comment in an elevator, a friend's offhand remark, or the line of a song from a passing radio ("Don't worry, be happy").

I like to think there are no accidents.

Positive lessons are not always taught in positive

> *The most important*
> *function of education*
> *at any level is to develop*
> *the personality of the individual*
> *and the significance of his life*
> *to himself and to others.*
> *This is the basic*
> *architecture of a life;*
> *the rest is ornamentation and*
> *decoration of the structure.*
>
> GRAYSON KIRK

ways. A flat tire (hardly a positive occurrence) can teach any number of lessons: acceptance, the value of planning, patience, the joy of service (if another person has the flat tire), the gratitude of being served (if another person helps you), and so on.

We can also use the same flat tire to learn (or relearn or rerelearn or—in my case—rererelearn) depressing lessons: life isn't fair; nothing can be trusted; if anything can go wrong it will (at the worst possible moment); life's a pain—then you die; nobody loves me.

Do you begin to see your role in all this? The classroom of life is not third grade, where all you will learn each day is neatly planned—including recess. In life, you *choose* what you learn from the many lessons presented to you, and your *choice* is fundamental to what you learn.

There are any number of lessons we can learn from any experience—both uplifting and "downpushing."

Experience, it is said, is the best teacher—providing, of course, we become the best students.

But who, really, is the teacher?

*We learn simply by the
exposure of living.
Much that passes for education
is not education at all
but ritual.
The fact is that we are
being educated when
we know it least.*

DAVID P. GARDNER

# Who Is the Real Teacher?

The real teacher of life is not experience. It's not overheard conversations or lines from songs or what you read in books (or the people who wrote the books).

The real teacher is *you*. You're the one who must decide, of all that comes your way, what is true and what is not, what applies to you and what does not, what you learn now and what you *promise yourself* you'll learn later.

Have you noticed that two people can read the same book or see the same movie or be in the same relationship and remember entirely different things? The best that life can do is *present* lessons to you. The learning is up to you.

I can't do any better than life. All I can do is present certain points of view, possible explanations, and whatever I have learned from certain experiences.

From what I present, it's up to you to say, "Yes, that fits," "No, that doesn't," or "Let me consider it for a while and see." If it fits, take it: it's yours. I just put words around something you already knew.

If you listen carefully, you'll hear (or sense) a voice inside you. It's the voice of your inner teacher. (I'll use the word *voice*, but for you it may be an image or a feeling or a sensation or any combination of these.) It may not be the loudest voice "in there," but it's often the most consistent, patient, and persistent one.

> *No matter how cynical you get,*
> *it is impossible to keep up.*
>
> LILY TOMLIN

What does your inner teacher sound like? It's the one that just said, "I sound like this."

If you're like me, you probably had other voices answering that question, too. "No, no, I sound like this." "There is no inner voice." "More than one voice? Do they think I'm crazy?" "Inner teacher. How stupid!"

But, through the din—lovingly, calmly, and perhaps a little amused by all the commotion caused by a simple question—the inner teacher reminds you,

"I am here. I have always been here. I'm on your side. I love you."

*As President Nixon says,*
*presidents can do*
*almost anything,*
*and President Nixon has done*
*many things that nobody*
*would have thought of doing.*

GOLDA MEIR

*Nobody can be*
*exactly like me.*
*Sometimes even I*
*have trouble doing it.*

TALLULAH BANKHEAD

# *Who* Are You?
# Who *Are* You?
# Who Are *You?*

What *are* all those other voices? Who's *saying* all that stuff? And why? And which "you" do I mean when I say, *"You* are the real teacher"?

Try a brief experiment. Take a moment and be aware of your body. Quickly "scan" it from your feet to your head. How does it feel? Are there any areas of tightness or tension? Do any parts feel particularly good? Is there any soreness or stiffness? Do you feel tired or alert?

Now, take a look at your emotions. (Or perhaps I should say, "Take a *feel* of your emotions.") What are you feeling? Excitement? Fear? Contentment? Irritability? Calmness? Emotions are often felt in and around the heart (the center of the chest) and the stomach. What are you feeling there?

One more bit of observation: notice your thoughts. What are you thinking? Listen to your mind as it goes through its thought process. A study once said we think at 1,200 words per minute. How they counted the words, I don't know. How they translated the visual and sensory thinking we do into words, I also don't know. That figure does, however, give a sense of the continual chatter going on in our brains. (Some Eastern traditions call this the "monkeymind.") Listen to the chatter for a moment.

> *When you close your doors,*
> *and make darkness within,*
> *remember never to say that*
> *you are alone,*
> *for you are not alone;*
> *nay, God is within,*
> *and your genius is within.*
> *And what need have they of light*
> *to see what you are doing?*
>
> EPICTETUS

Now, one question: Who did that? Who noticed the body? Who felt the feelings? Who observed the mind?

Maybe it was something other than the body, greater than the emotions, more magnificent than the mind.

Maybe it was *you*.

*Go directly*
*—see what she's doing,*
*and tell her she mustn't.*

1872

*The body is a community
made up of its innumerable
cells or inhabitants.*

Thomas Alva Edison

# Maybe You Are More
# Than Your Body

The body has enormous wisdom: it circulates blood, digests food, and performs thousands of necessary functions every second—all without your even having to "think" about them.

The body keeps itself from getting ill and heals itself when it does. It sees, hears, feels, tastes, smells—and has the sense to do that without ever being taught how. It performs the amazing feat of balancing itself on two legs, something—considering its size, proportions, and center of gravity—it has no business doing.

Alas, the body doesn't have much "smarts." Instincts, absolutely. Other animals have bodies, too—complete with wisdom and instincts. But something, whatever it is—reason, intelligence, awareness, soul, or "smarts"—separates humans from the rest of the animal kingdom.

Ask yourself: are you (the *you* you) located in the body, or located in the "something extra"? That's a loaded question, of course. Who can resist the temptation to associate themselves with "something extra" (especially a *mysterious* something extra)?

Even if we unload the question ("Are you more than your physical body?"), I think you see the point:

As remarkable as our bodies are, we somehow know that we are more remarkable than that.

**Crystal:** *Do you realize that most people use two percent of their mind's potential?*

**Roseanne:** *That much, huh?*

ROSEANNE

# Perhaps You Are More Than Your Mind

This is a difficult concept for thinkers to think about and for comprehenders to comprehend. "That which separates humans from beasts is the human being's superior intellect," they say, "its well-developed mind."

Perhaps, perhaps not. Let's explore.

The mind is often too full of opinions and "facts" about the way things *were* to accurately evaluate the way things *are*. For many people, the mind's job is to prove what it already knows is enough—there's no need to learn anything new.

As John Kenneth Galbraith pointed out, "Faced with the choice between changing one's mind and proving there is no need to do so, almost everyone gets busy on the proof."

Firmness of mind, to a point, is a good thing. It keeps us from being wishy-washy, swayed by every new tidbit of information that comes our way. If firmness is carried to an extreme, however, the mind becomes closed to new information from any source. The closed mind is, obviously, not open to learning. Learning is the assimilation and integration of new ideas, concepts, and behaviors.

You may be wondering, "Is my mind closed?" If you asked yourself that, it probably isn't. The closed mind, when faced with the concept that the mind is not the "It" of "Its," disregards the informa-

> *Your mind must always go,*
> *even while you're shaking hands*
> *and going through*
> *all the maneuvers.*
> *I developed the ability long ago*
> *to do one thing*
> *while thinking another.*
>
> RICHARD M. NIXON
>
> 1960

tion—often vehemently. (As Dorothy Parker said, "This book is not to be tossed lightly aside, but to be hurled with great force.")

If you're still reading this book and actively exploring the option that the mind might not be "you," then your mind is obviously open enough to accept the idea that it is not necessarily the It of Its, and therefore open to learning.

Books such as *LIFE 101* have filters built in—not into the book, but into the people who might read the book. Those not *open* to new ideas seldom read books that *contain* new ideas. These people don't even pick up such books—whose titles are often reason enough to disregard them. Their minds dismiss any book threatening to teach them something with, "It's one of *those* books."

Even certain sections in the bookstore are taboo. Some people never visit any of *those* sections. For some, the mere fact that it's a *book* is reason not to be bothered.

I don't mean to belittle the mind. (I make my living with mine.) The mind is an essential tool for sorting, organizing, conceptualizing, and replaying information.

My point is that the mind is a marvelous servant; it just makes a poor master.

*Joe, never feel guilty
about having
warm human feelings
toward anyone.*

BEN CARTWRIGHT

*BONANZA*

# Possibly You Are More Than Your Emotions

Feelings are good things to have—when you're feeling good. There's nothing that feels quite so good as good feelings. On the other hand, when feelings feel bad, we often wish we didn't feel at all.

Emotions are like the vibrations on the strings of a violin: they're essential to the song, but they're not the essence of the violin.

We experience life's pains and pleasures through our emotions. Because of this, some people decide they *are* their feelings—"I feel, therefore I am." The problem is, emotions are too often too wrong to be who we truly are.

Did you ever feel you could trust somebody and you couldn't? Did you ever feel something bad was going to happen and it didn't? Did you ever feel you could spend the rest of your life loving someone, and, well, you know what happened to that one. (or, more likely, you *don't* know what happened to that one.)

Our emotions are like yo-yo's: sometimes they're up, sometimes they're down. We can walk the dog, go 'round the world, or practice "sleeping." Yo-yo's are fun, but who's holding the string?

If someone's holding the string, then "you" must be more than the string—be it the string of a violin, the strings of your heart, or the string of a yo-yo.

*It's an
unanswered question,
but let us still believe in the
dignity and importance
of the question.*

TENNESSEE WILLIAMS

# So Who Are You?

If you're not your body, your mind, or your emotions, who are you?

Some might say our sense of self is simply an amalgam of the three; that the interplay of the body, mind, and emotions makes a whole that is greater than the sum of the parts, and that greater whole we call self.

This definition is fine with me—as are any religious, spiritual, or metaphysical views of self you may have. (I'll get to all those—yes, all of them—in just a moment.)

I'm not here to answer the question, "Who Are You?" I'm here to suggest that there is a "You" to be discovered. The discovery of that "You" is entirely your own—although the entire world is willing to help.

> **Jean-Paul Sartre**
> *(arriving in heaven):*
> *It's not what I expected.*
>
> **God:** *What did you expect?*
>
> **Sartre:** *Nothing.*
>
> *SCTV*

# The Gap: God, Religion, Reincarnation, Atheism, Agnosticism, and All That

I'm going to take a clear, unequivocal, unambiguous position on God, religion, reincarnation, atheism, agnosticism, and all that. My clear, unambiguous, and unequivocal position is this: I am clearly, unambiguously, unequivocally *not* taking a position.

It's not that I don't *have* a point of view about each of these; it's just that the information in *LIFE 101* works regardless of my or your or anyone's point of view.

There are certain forces—like the pull of gravity, the need for breathing, the desire for Häagen Dazs—that affect all of us regardless of beliefs. *LIFE 101* concerns itself with those "belief-proof" issues.

I'd like to introduce a portion of life I call The Gap. The Gap is the area into which I put the many (often conflicting) beliefs people have about What's The Big Force Behind It All And How Does This Big Force Interact With Human Beings?

The Gap can be any size, large or small. For some, it's a hairline crack; for others, it's vast enough to hold universes. I am not here to comment on the contents of anyone's Gap. The contents of your Gap are between you and whoever or whatever is in your Gap.

I am not confirming, endorsing, or supporting

> *I love God,*
> *and when you get to know Him,*
> *you find He's a Livin' Doll.*

JANE RUSSELL

*any* point of view. Most people will find this statement liberating. "You mean I don't have to sort out The Gap before I sort out my life?" No. In fact, a sorted, prosperous, joyful life might make Gap exploration all the more fruitful.

Some people have firm convictions on what should and should not be contained in everyone else's Gap. Others have powerful beliefs concerning the lack of the Gap itself. My militant wishy-washyism on this point will probably gather me detractors from both extremes.

One side might say, "I can't possibly read a book by a person who does not categorically and emphatically state that there is a God and believe in *my*

God *my* way." I might ask these people if they've ever read a cookbook, road atlas, or auto repair manual. These seldom state the theological convictions of the authors, but are nonetheless read by the righteous every day.

The other extreme might say, "I can't even consider a book by a person who is even *open* to the idea that there is a God." I wonder if these people also investigate the beliefs of their doctors, dentists, and mail carriers and refuse service if any of them happens to feel all right about the Almighty.

What *I* believe in is giving people the freedom to believe whatever they choose to believe. The techniques contained in *LIFE 101* will help believers, unbelievers, and everyone in between, to live a healthier, wealthier, and happier life.

I'll be discussing techniques as direct and mechanical as cooking, car repair, map reading, and mail delivery. Unlike cooking, car repair, map reading, and mail delivery, however, the techniques for living a happier, healthier, more productive life have, in some cases, been linked to specific religious (or nonreligious) beliefs.

What I'm attempting to do in this chapter is to separate these techniques (which work regardless of belief or disbelief) from the claim that organized schools of thought—be they "religious" or "scientific"—have, at times, placed upon them.

The doctor who gives a vaccination and says, "Thank God, this child is safe from smallpox," and the doctor who gives a vaccination and says, "Thank Jenner, this child is safe from smallpox,"

> *My religion consists*
> *of a humble admiration of the*
> *illimitable superior spirit*
> *who reveals himself*
> *in the slight details*
> *we are able to perceive with*
> *our frail and feeble mind.*
>
> ALBERT EINSTEIN

give the same vaccination. Some may say that the doctor who gives a blessing is a better doctor, and some may say that the doctor who sticks to medicine is a better doctor, but in either case—thank God and/or Jenner—the child is safe.

Historically, some religions have been slow to adopt certain "scientific" discoveries, and science has taken quite a while to adopt some "mystical" techniques.

Personally, I think we're all "old enough" to set aside the source, history, and trappings of certain techniques and ask of them a simple question: Do they work? (Do they produce the desired result? Do they get you what you want and need?)

In my thirty years of consciously exploring life (it started when I was fifteen, give or take a summer vacation), that's the question I've asked. (It's interesting that I can ask that question of itself, and it still holds up.)

So, as we go along, if I make a point that sounds like something you heard in Sunday school, that may be because you heard it in Sunday school. If I say something, and you think, "That sounds like the Ten Commandments," that may be because it's one of the Ten Commandments. If you say, "There he goes again, referring to Godless science," that's probably because I am referring, once again, to Godless science.

I care where ideas come from. I enjoy history. But I care even more where they might take me.

*Sooner or later every one
of us breathes an atom that
has been breathed before
by anyone you can think of
who has lived before us—
Michelangelo or
George Washington
or Moses.*

JACOB BRONOWSKI

# There Is More Going On Than Our Senses Perceive

Our view of the world is primarily made up of what we have perceived through our five senses. What we *personally* know of the world we have either seen, touched, tasted, smelled, or heard.

Unfortunately, our senses are limited; therefore our view of the world is limited. This is not a problem *unless* we start believing that what we perceive is all there is. It's not.

This can be disturbing news to those who believe, "If I can't see it, taste it, smell it, hear it, or feel it, forget it."

If I told you that, *right now,* there are hundreds of voices, pictures, and songs filling the air around you, but you are unable to see or hear any of them, what would you think?

Would you think I was talking some metaphysical mumbo jumbo? "If there were hundreds of voices, pictures, and songs around me, I'd be able to at least see or hear *some* of them."

Not necessarily.

"Then your explanation's going to be pretty weird."

Not necessarily.

"Okay, so explain."

Right now you are surrounded by waves of energy...

"I knew it would be weird."

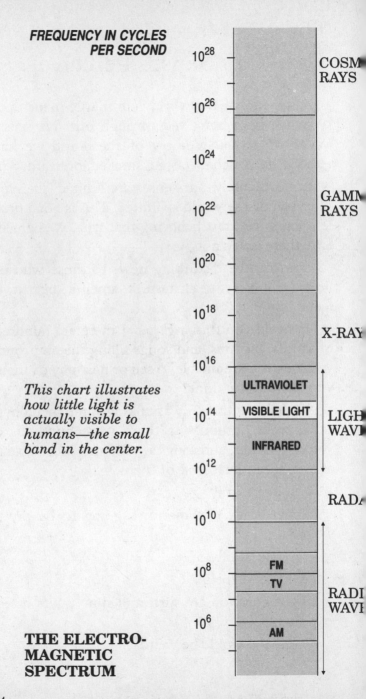

**FREQUENCY IN CYCLES PER SECOND**

$10^{28}$

COSM
RAYS

$10^{26}$

$10^{24}$

GAMM
RAYS

$10^{22}$

$10^{20}$

$10^{18}$

X-RAY

$10^{16}$

ULTRAVIOLET

*This chart illustrates how little light is actually visible to humans—the small band in the center.*

$10^{14}$

VISIBLE LIGHT

LIGH
WAVI

INFRARED

$10^{12}$

$10^{10}$

RAD/

FM

$10^{8}$

TV

RADI
WAVI

$10^{6}$

AM

**THE ELECTRO-MAGNETIC SPECTRUM**

...that are used to transmit radio, television, walkie-talkie, CB, portable telephone, and many other communication devices. The reason you don't know they're there is because your senses are unable to perceive these signals.

If you had, say, a TV, you could "tune in" these waves of energy. The TV would translate what your senses cannot perceive into what they can. The fact that we can't see, hear, or feel these waves without a TV doesn't mean they're not there.

And so it is with all sorts of natural and human-made phenomena: if we have the proper instruments, we can perceive them; if not, we can't.

Dogs smell and hear better than most humans. Cats see better in the dark. Birds are more sensitive to movement. Even houseflies seem to "know" when you're about to swat them.*

The point is simple: there is more to life than meets the eye.

*Did you know that houseflies take off *backwards?* If you want to swat one, aim slightly *behind* it. See? This book is just *full* of things you never learned in school.

*Man is slightly nearer
to the atom than to the star.
From his central position
man can survey
the grandest works of Nature
with the astronomer,
or the minutest works
with the physicist.*

SIR ARTHUR STANLEY

# The Great Pretender, or, *All* Life Is in the Fast Lane

Let's—just for the heck of it—break life into its component parts; or, maybe, part. When we decide to "get small," atoms are a good place to start.

To get an idea of how small an atom is, imagine a cherry. Then imagine trillions and trillions of cherries, all in one enormous ball. Imagine a ball the size of the earth, all made up of cherries.

This large ball of cherries the size of the earth would be a fairly accurate model of the atomic structure of an orange. That is, if you enlarged an orange until it was the size of the earth, the atoms in that very big orange would be the size of cherries. And the cherries would be so far apart, you could see right through it.

Another demonstration of an atom's smallness: pure gold can be pounded very thin. When pounded extremely thin, it's known as gold leaf. Gold leaf is about five gold atoms thick. If this book, and three others just as thick, were printed on gold leaf, the total thickness of all four books would be about as thick as a single sheet of paper.

Remember those models of atoms they showed us in school? They looked like little solar systems. (In some schools, they probably used the same model for both atoms *and* solar systems.) In the middle were the protons and neutrons; this, the teacher explained, formed the nucleus. Then, only slightly smaller than the nucleus, and about twelve

> *A physicist is an atom's way*
> *of knowing about atoms.*
>
> GEORGE WALD

inches away, dangling at the end of what looked like a coat hanger wire, was the electron.

In fact, the whole "solar system" model of an atom has been abandoned. Think of the proton and neutron in the center, surrounded by a *cloud*. That cloud would be the electron (or electrons) of the atom.

In addition, the *scale* of the high-school model was, to say the least, inaccurate. If the nucleus of the atom were, say, the size of a tennis ball, the electron cloud would be from one to ten *miles* thick in all directions (depending on the size of the atom). If the nucleus were the size of a tennis ball, the atom would be from two to twenty miles in diameter.

To give you another idea of the size: imagine the dome of St. Peter's Cathedral in Rome. (If you haven't been to St. Peter's, imagine the biggest dome you have ever seen and make it bigger.) If a hydrogen atom were the size of St. Peter's dome, the nucleus would be the size of a grain of salt.

But an atom with a nucleus the size of a grain of salt only *appears to be* the size of St. Peter's dome. The nucleus is 99.95 percent of the mass ("solid stuff") of the atom. The rest of the atom is nothing, appearing to be much, much more—a grain of salt pretending to be a dome.

The *Encyclopædia Britannica* tells us, "An atom (and thus all matter) is mostly empty space."

How does an atom do this? *Energy.* The protons and neutrons in the nucleus of the atom move about at 40,000 miles per *second.* The electron cloud is full of (not surprisingly) *electrical* energy.

Not only is the empty space *within* atoms large, but the space *between* atoms—the space in which there is nothing at all—is enormous.

This doesn't fit our perception of—or even belief about—things at all. As *Britannica* tells us, "Some daily life concepts are no longer valid on the atomic scale." Indeed.

For example, there is more empty space in the book you're holding than book. The atoms of the book give the *illusion* of solid ink on solid paper.

They're not. It's just an illusion. If the electricity in the electron cloud were switched off, even for an

> *The important thing in science is*
> *not so much to obtain new facts*
> *as to discover new ways*
> *of thinking about them.*
>
> Sir William Bragg

instant, this book would crumble into atomic dust—an amount of dust not even visible to the naked eye. This book would appear to disappear. Poof.

The same is true of whatever you're sitting (or lying) on, everything in the room or vehicle you're currently in, and everything you've ever seen, touched, heard, tasted, or smelled.

It is also, by the way, true of your body.

Welcome to life.

*The most incomprehensible thing
about the world is that
it is comprehensible.*

ALBERT EINSTEIN

*Any sufficiently
advanced technology
is indistinguishable
from magic.*

ARTHUR C. CLARKE

# What Did That Last Chapter Mean, Anyway?

So what does a chapter on atomic physics have to do with a book on life? A few facts can be gleaned from the study of the atom:

1. Contrary to our perception and belief, there is more nothing than something, even in things that appear to have more something than nothing.

2. Everything is always in motion, even things that don't appear to have moved in millions of years.

3. The perception that things are solid and stationary is an illusion.

Physicist Fritjof Capra, in *The Tao of Physics:*

> As we penetrate into matter, nature does not show us any isolated "basic building blocks," but rather appears as a complicated web of relations between the various parts of the whole. These relations always include the observer in an essential way. The human observer constitutes the final link in the chain of the observational processes, and the properties of any atomic object can be understood only in terms of the object's interaction with the observer.

Capra concludes, "In atomic physics, we can never speak of nature without, at the same time, speaking of ourselves."

Life, it turns out, is not a struggle; it's a wiggle.

# Which Is More Important— Heredity or Eliot?

Remember the old question: "Which is more important—heredity or environment?" I say *old* question when, perhaps, I should say *obsolete* question. The question *has* been answered and, in time, will be asked about as often as "Is the world flat or round?" "Is sex possible after forty?" "Does McDonald's 'do it all for you,' or do they do it all for money?"

The answers to these questions (in order) are: heredity, round, I don't remember, and money.

An elaborate study tracked down identical twins separated at birth. Each twin had grown up in a different environment, but had the same genetics. In some cases, the environments were *very* different—one twin grew up in poverty, the other in luxury; one with stern parents, the other with permissive parents; one in a devoutly religious family, the other in a devoutly indifferent family; one in a "broken" home, the other in a "happy" home. Some were even raised in other cultures and grew up speaking different native languages.

The twins were given tests that measured more than one hundred variables of personality. What the study found was that the identical twins were, in a word, identical—they were, essentially, the *same person*.

Yes, of course, each had individual distinctions—just as there is *something* that distinguishes

> *With me,*
> *it's just a genetic*
> *dissatisfaction with everything.*
>
> WOODY ALLEN

one seagull from another—but, when compared to other people (like comparing seagulls to skylarks), identical twins were far more the same than different.

A seagull is a seagull is a seagull, a rose is a rose is a rose, you are you are you.* This study merely supports numerous other studies that have gradually, gradually, gradually traced the "roots" of who we are to younger and younger ages. Studies indi-

---

*Let's all sing along: "Old McWilliams wrote a book / URURU. / And in this book / he said with pride / 'IMIMI'." Enough singing—back to class.

cated the basic personality was formed before puberty, then before age five, then before two, then sometime between the first Lamaze class and the father's yelling: "I can't take any more of this! I need something for the pain!"

In one human trait after another, what was once considered a "choice" now is seen as the result of the birth-parents' tossing the old genetic dice. Such characteristics as body weight, sexual preference, and shopping at K-Mart seem to be as genetically based as eye color, height, and intelligence. Yes, we can "choose" to go against genetics but usually with great difficulty. K-Mart shoppers are simply never going to be happy shopping exclusively at Neiman Marcus—and vice versa. (Especially vice versa. More vice versa than verse vica.)

Yes, severe extremes in the environment will override genetics—extended malnutrition in childhood, for example, can stunt growth, just as extreme societal prejudice can make those with more than the "normal" number of fat cells near-anorexic or make homosexuals mimic heterosexuality.*

"But studies prove that troubled youths come from troubled homes." Yes, troubled youths *are*

---

*The latter two examples have as much to do with the individuals' need for approval and their willingness to conform as they do with social pressures. There are, after all, any number of happy heavy people and gay homosexuals. The need for approval and willingness to conform, however, are most likely, yes, genetic.

> *What more felicity*
> *can fall to creature,*
> *Than to enjoy delight*
> *with liberty.*
>
> EDMUND SPENSER
> *THE FATE OF THE BUTTERFLY*
>
> 1591

more likely to come from troubled homes just as chickens tend to come from chicken coops, but that doesn't mean troubled homes create troubled youths any more than chicken coops create chickens. Troubled youths come from troubled homes because they inherited troubled genes from the troubled homemakers.

Frankly, the common belief that environment is more important than heredity—or even that the two are equally important—is but another example of our habit, as humans, of setting ourselves above nature. We are a *part* of nature. We grow *from* it; we're not placed *in* it. Consequently, the laws of nature apply to us as much as they apply to snowflakes, water buffalo, and Spam. And one of nature's most fundamental laws is that of genetics. Plant a radish seed; get a radish.

If you're an orange blossom, don't look forward to being an apple. If you're a rose, you come with thorns.

All of this came home—literally—when I ordered a see-the-miracle-of-nature-and-grow-your-own-butterflies kit. A week later the UPS driver delivered a plastic cup with some green gunk on the bottom and on top of the green gunk were five black, half-inch-long pipe-cleaners. The pipe cleaners, I discovered, were caterpillars. *These things* were going to become butterflies? Yeah, right.

The black pipe cleaners moved around and ate the green gunk and got bigger. I was still quite certain I had been sent the grow-your-own-pipe-cleaners kit by mistake.

After about ten days—as if someone had rung a bell—all the caterpillars climbed to the top of the cup, attached themselves to the lid, and promptly turned into chrysalises. On each chrysalis was gold—iridescent, reflective, shiny *gold!* How on earth did black pipe-cleaners eating green gunk make *gold?*

No time to marvel, because B-Day was on its way, and I had to put together the supplied butterfly house "which any child can assemble in less than thirty minutes." Of course, it took me half a day, and even then I had to accept the fact that my butterflies were going to be raised in substandard housing. (I never did find tab "C" which was supposed to

> *The butterfly glow*
> *in the narrow flute from which*
> *the morning-glory opens*
> *blue and cool on a hot morning.*
>
> DENISE LEVERTOV

go into slot "K.")

Into their new slum housing went the chrysalises, out of which, after another ten days and another inaudible (to me) alarm bell—came *butterflies*.
Painted lady butterflies. On the wings were every
color of the rainbow. How on earth did every color
of the rainbow come from black caterpillars eating
green gunk?

The answer to "how on earth?" is that they are
*of* the earth. That's just what painted lady caterpillars *do*. It's in their genetic code. It's determined the
moment the egg is fertilized. It's not just when and
how to turn from black pipe-cleaner to iridescent
gold chrysalis to multicolored butterfly; the code

also includes what to eat, how to eat, how to mate, when to mate, and when and where to migrate.

My gracious—migration. Painted lady butterflies gather by the millions—again at a time determined by one of those inaudible bells—and fly south together—often more than *two thousand miles!* In the spring, they gather again and fly back home.

All the painted lady butterfly needs to know— from eating to migrating to making other painted lady butterflies—is contained within the fertilized egg. It's run by the law of genetics—as is almost every other portion of the living world. Even us.

Perhaps I should say *especially* us. Imagine all the painted lady butterfly "knows" before it even hatches itself; then imagine how much more *we* must "know" with our more intricate and elaborate genetic make-up. Yes, we are different from butterflies—not because we *chose* to be different, but because we *are* different.

Are human beings superior to butterflies? It depends on your criteria. When it comes to eating three hot dogs in less than five minutes, humans are far superior to butterflies. But when it comes to flying . . .*

---

*The pipe cleaners and green gunk—along with build-it-yourself-substandard-butterfly housing—are available from Insect Lore Products, P. O. Box 1535, Shafter, CA 93263. I do *not* get a royalty. I will *not* be making an infomercial for them. I'll leave that to Cher.

> *I do not know whether*
> *I was then a man dreaming*
> *I was a butterfly,*
> *or whether I am now a butterfly*
> *dreaming I am a man.*

> CHUANG-TZU
>
> 369–286 B.C.

**PAINTED LADY LESSON #1:**

The only reasonable course of action seems to be acceptance.

**PAINTED LADY LESSON #2:**

Yes, we *can* make change, but change is *very* expensive and our resources *are* limited. *Choose wisely* what to change; accept the rest.

**PAINTED LADY LESSON #3:**

Eat the green gunk, hang in there, listen for the alarm bells, and there will be golden, fluttering, soaring surprises.

**PAINTED LADY LESSON #4:**

It is easier to wear and improve the genes you

already have than to go to the Gap and try to get another pair.

Does this mean be complacent? Not at all. There is so much *not* inherited; so much to be *learned*. All the great thoughts of those who went before, for example. T. S. Eliot wrote that tradition "cannot be inherited, and if you want it you must obtain it by great labor" (Some of that "great labor" might include deciphering the works of T. S. Eliot. He is, by his own admission, "Full of high sentence, but a bit obtuse." Like all good learning, however, understanding Eliot *is* worth the effort).

> Poets in our civilization, as it exists at present, must be *difficult*....The poet must become more and more comprehensive, more allusive, more indirect, in order to force, to dislocate if necessary, language into its meaning.

But, Eliot continues: "Genuine poetry can communicate before it is understood." That's a relief. Capturing the poem is not:

> Each venture
> Is a new beginning, a raid on the inarticulate
> With shabby equipment always deteriorating
> In the general mess of imprecision of feeling.

One cannot write poetry for fame, and certainly not for *money*. (What are the odds Andrew Lloyd Webber will take *your* poetry and turn it into *Cats?*)

> As things are, and as fundamentally they must always be, poetry is not a career, but a mug's game.

> *Poetry is not an assertion of truth,*
> *but the making of that truth*
> *more real to us.*
>
> T. S. Eliot

No honest poet can ever feel quite sure of the permanent value of what he has written: he may have wasted his time and messed up his life for nothing.

Well, let's take a glimpse at this mug's game. (Each paragraph is an excerpt from an Eliot poem—my apologies to Eliot for their selection and arrangement.)

> Wavering between the profit and the loss
> In this brief transit where the dreams cross
> The dreamcrossed twilight
> between birth and dying.

Where is the Life we have lost in living?
Where is the wisdom we have lost in knowledge?
Where is the knowledge we have lost in information?


The readers of the *Boston Evening Transcript*
Sway in the wind like a field of ripe corn.


What is hell?
Hell is oneself,
Hell is alone, the other figures in it
Merely projections.


I have measured out my life with coffee spoons.


Who then devised the torment? Love.
Love is the unfamiliar Name
Behind the hands that wove
The intolerable shirt of flame
Which human power cannot remove.
We only live, only suspire
Consumed by either fire or fire.


Uncorseted, her friendly bust
Gives promise of pneumatic bliss.


   Between the conception and the creation
Between the emotion and the response
Falls the Shadow.


   And indeed there will be time
To wonder, "Do I dare?" and, "Do I dare?"

> *It is eternity now.*
> *I am in the midst of it.*
> *It is about me in the sunshine;*
> *I am in it,*
> *as the butterfly*
> *in the light-laden air.*
> *Nothing has to come;*
> *it is now.*
> *Now is eternity;*
> *now is the immortal life.*
>
> RICHARD JEFFRIES
>
> 1883

Between the idea
And the reality
Between the motion
And the act
Falls the Shadow

Stand on the highest pavement of the stair—
Lean on a garden urn—
Weave, weave the sunlight in your hair.

Let us go then, you and I,
When the evening is spread out against the sky
Like a patient etherized upon a table.

O hidden under the dove's wing,
hidden in the turtle's breast,
Under the palmtree at noon,
under the running water
At the still point of the turning world.
O hidden.

Except for the point, the still point,
There would be no dance,
and there is only the dance.

We shall not cease from exploration
And the end of all our exploring
Will be to arrive where we started
And know the place for the first time.

≈

Note how this chapter metamorphosed?
'Tis but a gift of butterflies.

*The only good is knowledge
and the only evil
is ignorance.*

SOCRATES

# Are Human Beings Fundamentally Good or Fundamentally Evil?

My answer: good.

My proof? I could quote philosophers, psychologists, and poets, but then those who believe humans are fundamentally evil can quote just as many philosophers, psychologists, and poets.

My proof, such as it is, is a simple one. It returns to the source of human life: an infant.

When you look into the eyes of an infant, what do you see? I've looked into a few, and I have yet to see fundamental evil radiating from a baby's eyes. There seems to be purity, joy, brightness, splendor, sparkle, marvel, happiness—you know: good.

And yet, if we are fundamentally good, why is it when we relax and listen to our thoughts or feel our emotions or sense our bodies, we often find so much rubbish? Here's my explanation for that, in the form of a diagram.

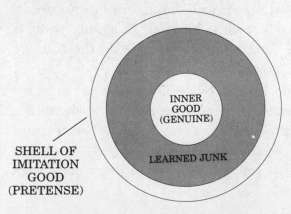

INNER GOOD (GENUINE)

LEARNED JUNK

SHELL OF IMITATION GOOD (PRETENSE)

> *When choosing*
> *between two evils,*
> *I always like to try*
> *the one I've never tried before.*
>
> MAE WEST

Babies are like sponges; they absorb everything. By the time they are two years old, they have observed more than 8,000 hours of life: the good, the bad, the ugly—plus whatever was on TV.

As they begin to act out this array of observations, they are informed—sometimes in no uncertain terms—that some behavior is "good," some is "bad," and "around here we don't do the bad, we only do the good."

What do I mean by "evil?" Evil is unnecessary life experience. Whatever we *need* to do to learn a lesson is *life*—even if it's "not fun." When the not-fun continues after the lesson is learned—or the job is done—that's evil. To cut off a dog's tail (when necessary) is life. To do it an inch at a time is evil.

At first, the child has trouble understanding why some things are "right" while others are "wrong." (This stage is often referred to as the Terrible Twos.) But, eventually the child learns—with varying degrees of success—to cover the bad with the good, the wrong with the right.

We are taught to pretend to be good, and when we let the pretense slip, we find evil lurking just below the surface. It's little wonder, then, that most people think their inner self is bad. The struggle to keep up the "good act" is a "never-ending battle for truth, justice, and the American Way."

When people have the patience (and courage) to go beneath the "inner evil," they find, invariably, a sea of peace, calm, and joy. They have reached the inner good that is their true nature.

Ironically, this inner good is often remarkably similar to the "good shell" that was fabricated for them by the Parental Construction Company. The difference here is that, coming from this center, people do good because good is the thing to do, not because they're "supposed to" do good, or because they might get punished if they don't.

Your friends may think you're, say, a happy person. You might think, "What do they know? If only they knew how unhappy I am inside. I only *pretend* to be happy, and they fall for it. What kind of friends are these?" The truth may be that beneath the unhappiness is a genuine happiness—and perhaps the happiness your friends see is the genuine happiness, not the pretense of happiness you use as

> *Good people are good*
> *because they've come*
> *to wisdom through failure.*
>
> WILLIAM SAROYAN

a cover.

This is true of any "good" emotion, thought, or behavior: love, joy, gratitude, enthusiasm, compassion, generosity, tenderness, bravery, cleanliness, reverence, and all the rest.

If you think you're fooling people with your act of goodness, and you think you aren't all that good, maybe the one you're fooling is yourself.

*Man's main task in life
is to give birth
to himself,
to become what he
potentially is.*

ERICH FROMM

*Be wiser than
other people,
if you can,
but do not
tell them so.*

LORD CHESTERFIELD

# PART TWO

## ADVANCED TOOLS FOR EAGER LEARNERS

Life is, if nothing else, a persistent teacher. It will repeat a lesson over and over until it is learned. How does life know we've learned? When we change our behavior. Until then, even if we intellectually "know" something, we haven't really *learned* it. School remains in session.

The good news is that we learn all we need to know—eventually.

For some, however, eventually is not soon enough. If there's something they can learn that will *eventually* make their lives happier, healthier, and more productive, why not learn it *now*? That brings happiness, health, and productivity to us sooner—and it avoids a lot of (perhaps painful) lessons along the way.

Others aren't content with learning only what they "need" to know. "Getting by" is not enough. They want more. They are the "eager learners" who read books with titles such as *LIFE 101*.

Someone once said that the only two things that motivate an enlightened person are love and curiosity. I can't speak for my state of enlightenment, but

> *What a wonderful*
> *day we've had.*
> *You have learned something,*
> *and I have learned something.*
> *Too bad we didn't*
> *learn it sooner.*
> *We could have*
> *gone to the movies instead.*
>
> BALKI BARTOKOMOUS

I can say that, considering my level of curiosity, it's a good thing I'm not a cat.

Anatole France pointed out more than a century ago, "The whole art of teaching is only the art of awakening the natural curiosity of young minds for the purpose of satisfying it afterwards."

But what if we have questions that seemingly can't be answered? When faced with this quandary, I like to comfort myself with this thought of Emerson: "Undoubtedly we have no questions to ask which are unanswerable. We must trust the perfection of the creation so far as to believe that whatever curiosity the order of things has awakened in our minds, the order of things can satisfy."

"Life was meant to be lived," Eleanor Roosevelt wrote in her autobiography, "and curiosity must be kept alive. One must never, for whatever reason, turn his back on life."

This section of the book contains a series of tools designed to keep curiosity alive and thriving. These same tools can also be used to find satisfying answers to the questions you may be curious about. These techniques are designed to accelerate the process of learning.

All of these tools, by the way, are optional. To learn the necessary lessons of life, no one *needs* to know or use any of them. So there's no need to struggle—thinking that if you don't master them your life will be a failure. Experiment with these techniques. Play with them. Have fun.

Also, there's no need to teach these techniques to anyone else—much less *insist* that people relate to you as though they've already mastered them. These skills are electives in the school of life. If you choose to use any or all of them for *your* accelerated learning, that's fine; but please don't expect—and certainly don't demand—that others accelerate their learning too.

Before we start, let's take a look at why human beings spend so much time struggling *against* learning; why we, as a species, seem so opposed to the exploration of new things.

Haven't you been curious about that?

*The only reason I always
try to meet and know
the parents better
is because it helps me
to forgive their children.*

LOUIS JOHANNOT

# Why Do We Resist Learning?

If we're here to learn, and if we have this seemingly in-built desire to learn (curiosity), why do we resist learning? The classic example is the argument: "Listen to me!" "No, you listen to me!" "No, you listen to me!" And so on.

It seems that somewhere around eighteen (give or take ten years), something in us decides, "That's it, I've had it, I'm done. I know all I need to know. I'm not learning any more."

Why?

Let's return to the idea of the small child being taught about life by his or her parents. Parents are like gods to little children—the source of food, protection, comfort, love.

Also, parents are BIG! They're four to five times bigger than children. Imagine how much respect (awe? fear?) you'd have for someone twenty to thirty feet tall, weighing 500 to 1,000 pounds.

Let's imagine a child—two, three years old—playing in a room. The parents are reading, the child is playing, all is well. After an hour or so, CRASH! The child bumps a table and knocks over a lamp.

Where there once was almost no interaction with the parents, suddenly there is a lot—almost all of it negative. "How many times have we told you…." "Can't you do anything right?" "What's the matter with you?" "That was my favorite lamp!" Shame, bad, nasty, no good. This verbal tirade may

> *I have found the best way*
> *to give advice to your children*
> *is to find out what they want*
> *and then advise them to do it.*
>
> HARRY S. TRUMAN

or may not be reinforced by physical punishment.

What does the child remember from an evening at home with the folks? Does the child remember the hours spent successfully playing (i.e., no broken anything) while Mommy and Daddy read, or does he or she remember the intense ten minutes of "bad boy," "nasty girl," "shame, shame, shame," after the fall?

The negative, of course. It was loud and it was frightening (imagine a pair of thirty-foot, 1,000-pound gods yelling at you). It was, for the most part, the *only* interaction the child may have had with "the gods" all evening. (Especially if being put to bed early was part of the punishment.)

When a child's primary memory of the communication from his or her parents ("the gods") is "no, don't, stop that, shouldn't, mustn't, shame, bad, bad, bad," what's the child being taught? That he or she can do no good; must be alert for failure at every moment, and still will fail; is a disappointment, a letdown, a failure.

In short, a child begins to believe that he or she is fundamentally not good enough, destined for failure, in the way. In a word, *unworthy*.

There is very little in the traditional educational system to counteract this mistaken belief. If anything, school etches the image even deeper. (If we learned all we needed to know in kindergarten, it was promptly drummed out of us in first grade.) You are taught you must perform, keep up, and "make the grade," or you aren't worth much. If you *do* work hard at making the grades, some authority figure is bound to ask, "Why are you studying all the time? Why aren't you out playing with the other children? What's wrong with you? Don't you have any friends?"

Catch-22 never had it so good.

Naturally, we can't go around feeling unworthy *all the time*. It hurts too much. So we invent defenses—behaviors that give the *illusion* of safety. Soon we notice that others have not only adopted similar defenses, but have taken their defenses to new and exotic extremes. The school of limitation is in session.

We begin hanging out with other members of the same club. We are no longer alone. In fact, we

> *I was thrown out of college*
> *for cheating*
> *on the metaphysics exam;*
> *I looked into the soul*
> *of the boy next to me.*
>
> WOODY ALLEN

start to feel worthy. We have comrades, companions, confidants, and chums.

The club? Club Let's-Hide-Away-From-The-Hurtful-Unworthiness International has four main chapters:

## The Rebels

The rebels like to think of themselves as "independent." They have, in fact, merely adopted a knee-jerk reaction to whatever "law" is set before them. They are prime candidates for reverse psychology. ("The best way to keep children from putting beans in their ears is to tell them they *must* put beans in their ears.") They conform to nonconformity.

**MOST FEARED FORTUNE COOKIE:** "A youth should be respectful to his elders."

**SLOGAN:** "Authority, you tell us that we're no good. Well, authority, *you're* no good."

**MOTTO** (minus the first two words): "...and the horse you came in on!"
If the ones who tell you you're no good are no good, then, somehow, that makes you good. Somehow.

## The Unconscious

These are the people who seem to be not all there because, for the most part, they're not all there. They're not dumb, mind you; they're just someplace else: a desert island, a rock concert, an ice cream parlor. They are masters of imagination. With authority figures, they do their best to *appear* dumb, drugged, or asleep. The powers that be then become frustrated and leave them alone—precisely what the unconscious want. Very clever.

**FAVORITE FORTUNE COOKIE:** "To know that you do not know is the best."

**SLOGAN:** "You can't expect much from me, so you can't criticize me because, uh, um, what was I saying?"

**MOTTO:** "Huh?"
The more the world criticizes them, the more they retreat to a fantasy world beyond criticism.

> *A boy becomes an adult*
> *three years before*
> *his parents think he does,*
> *and about two years after*
> *he thinks he does.*
>
> LEWIS B. HERSHEY

## The Comfort Junkies

All that is (or might be) uncomfortable is avoided (unless avoiding it would be more uncomfortable), and all that might bring comfort (food, TV, Walkmans, drink, drugs, and other distractions) is sought after (unless the seeking after them would be more uncomfortable). In their youth the comfort junkies scarf french fries, then mature into couch potatoes.

**MOST FEARED FORTUNE COOKIE:** "The scholar who cherishes the love of comfort is not fit to be deemed a scholar."

**SLOGAN:** "Comfort at any cost! (Unless it's too

expensive.)"

**MOTTO** (taken from Tolkien): "In a hole in the ground there lived a hobbit. Not a nasty, dirty, wet hole, filled with the ends of worms and an oozy smell, nor yet a dry, bare, sandy hole with nothing in it to sit down on or to eat: it was a hobbit-hole, and that means comfort."

They memorize as much of their motto as is comfortable.

## The Approval Seekers

The best way to prove worthiness is to have lots of people telling you how wonderful you are. Approval seekers work so hard for other people's approval they have little or no time to seek their own. But their own doesn't matter. They, after all, are unworthy, and what's the worth of an unworthy person's opinion? These people take the opposite tack of the rebels: rebels deem the opinions of others unworthy; approval seekers deem others' opinions *too* worthy. Approval seekers would run for class president, but they're afraid of a backlash, so they usually win treasurer by a landslide.

**MOST FEARED FORTUNE COOKIE:** "Fine words and an insinuating appearance are seldom associated with true virtue."

**SLOGAN:** "What can I do for *you* today?"

**MOTTO:** "Nice sweater!"

Without such people, homecoming floats would never get built.

> *I'm an experienced woman;*
> *I've been around...*
> *Well, all right,*
> *I might not've been around,*
> *but I've been...nearby.*
>
> MARY RICHARDS
> *THE MARY TYLER MOORE SHOW*

You've probably been able to place all your friends in their respective clubhouses. If you're having trouble placing yourself, you might ask a few friends.*

Most of us tend to pay some dues to each chap-

---

*If you reject the idea that you could possibly fit into any category, you're probably a rebel. If you accept your friends' evaluations too readily, you may be looking for approval. If you forget to ask, maybe you're unconscious. If you're afraid to ask, you may be seeking comfort. If a friend says, "You don't fit in any of these; you seem to transcend them all," that person is probably looking for *your* approval.

ter at one time or another, about one aspect of life or another. We may, for example, be rebels when it comes to speed limits, unconscious when it comes to income tax, comfort junkies when it comes to our favorite bad habit, and approval seekers in intimate relationships.

These are also the four major ways people avoid learning. The rebels don't need to learn; the unconscious don't remember why they should; the comfortable find it too risky; and the approval seekers don't want to rock any boats. Most of us have our own personal combination of the four—a little of this and a little of that—that has perhaps kept us from learning all we'd like to know.

How to surmount these ancient barriers? Tools, techniques, and practice, practice, practice. Where do we find these tools? The rest of this book has quite a few.

*Rule #1:*
*Don't sweat*
*the small stuff.*


*Rule #2:*
*It's all small stuff.*


DR. MICHAEL MANTELL

# Rules as Tools

One of the most effective tools for eager learners is one of the oldest—and one of the first to be resisted—*rules*.

As soon as we were able—as late as two years old for late-bloomers—we learned how to get around rules. In most cases, rules were treated as the *enemy*, something laid out by an impersonal (and perhaps tyrannical) world, designed to limit us, punish us, or upset us.

It's easy to see how rules could be thought of as the enemy. From a child's point of view, if there were no rules, our parents would never be upset with us. Only when a rule was violated did they withdraw their love. If those rules weren't there, our parents would always love us. Or so goes the logic of a child.

Further, it seemed as though rules were some sort of childhood curse, like chicken pox, mumps, or measles. Adults got to stay up late and watch TV. Adults got to eat two desserts. Adults got to cross the street. Adults never had to take afternoon naps. "When *can* I do this?" we would ask. "When you're older," we were told.

Rules, we figured, were some temporary malady—like chicken pox or siblings—we had to endure. One fine day, it would all be over. Imagine our surprise as we grew older—three, four, five—when we found that the number and complexity of rules actually *increased*.

> *Is forbidden*
> *to steal towels, please.*
> *If you are not person to do such*
> *is please not to read notice.*
>
> SIGN IN TOKYO HOTEL

Then came that repository of rules itself: school. After the initial shock, we gulped and, to one degree or another, accepted our fate: The rules will continue, unabated, for twelve more years. *Then* they will be over.

Hardly. Many of the childhood rules were internalized—they didn't go away, they just became habits. We didn't play in traffic, not because it was a rule, but because we knew the consequences of playing in traffic. We didn't stay up all night watching TV because we knew how we'd feel in the morning. We didn't have two desserts because— well, maybe we did. But we knew what it would do, and it did.

The confusion about rules when we were young was that some rules were useful to us, and some were not. We were, however, expected to follow *all* of them *or else*. In time, rules we found useful were no longer rules; they became part of us. The ones that didn't become a part of us were "rules," and we hated them (or forgot about them or ignored them or followed them for approval—or some combination of these).

Take walking, for example. Walking is full of rules. Considering the size of our feet and the height of our body, human beings have no business standing at all. Try to get a Barbie doll (or G.I. Joe) to stand up without support—especially in heels. (G.I. Joe has a *very* difficult time in heels.)

If we forget any of the rules of walking, gravity exacts its "punishment." It is swift, unerring, and consistent. So we learn the rules of walking, and we make those rules our own.

The same is true of language, use of our hands, general body coordination, and so on. All the things we weren't born doing, we had to learn. Each has its own set of rules. Once we mastered the rules and made them our own, we forgot the rules and just did it.

Some rules are absolute, some arbitrary. "Keep breathing" is absolute. "Drive on the right side of the road in North America" is arbitrary. There's no special *reason* to drive on the right side of the road—approximately half the world drives on the left. The reason it's a "good" rule is that, as long as everybody follows it, it works. We don't have to

> *Exit according to rule,*
> *first leg and then head.*
> *Remove high heels and synthetic*
> *stockings before evacuation:*
> *Open the door,*
> *take out the recovery line*
> *and throw it away.*
>
> RUMANIAN NATIONAL AIRLINES
> EMERGENCY INSTRUCTIONS

decide every time we pass an oncoming car which way to pass it. It saves time, attention, worry, and lives.

Sometimes rule-following is part of "paying your dues." You may know a better way of doing something—that is, you may have a new rule that's better than the old one—but in order to implement the improved rule, you have to follow the old rule for a while. Once you master the old rule, you are then the master—and masters get to change things. Once you're successful at something, to do it another way is considered innovative. If you've yet to master the old way, it's often seen as rebellion.

I'm certainly not saying "Conform and you'll be

happy." To change rules that are already in place takes time, energy, perseverance, and a lot of hard work. You only have so many of these assets at your disposal, so choose with care the rules you want to change.

What I'm suggesting is that you change your *view* of rules. This book is full of "rules." If you treat them the way many people treat rules—with rebellion, unconsciousness, discomfort, or as new ways to gain others' acceptance—these techniques I'm suggesting will probably not be very useful. They'll just be more "should's," "must's," "ought-to's," and "have-to's."

As I mentioned before, I'm suggesting that you take each suggestion as a suggestion, try it out, see if it works. If it does, use it. Then it's a *tool,* not a rule. If it doesn't, let it go and move on to something that may. Then it's not a rule; it's just a tool that, for whatever reason, you have no use for at this time.

Here are three rules I have found to be the foundation for all the other rules I have adopted for myself. If *rules* is too strong a word, consider them perhaps *guidelines.* They're simple, but I've found that the challenges within them never seem to end.

**1. Don't hurt yourself and don't hurt others.** This begins at the physical level: don't hit people, don't steal from them, don't hit yourself on the head with a hammer. These are fairly easy to define. Then it moves to a more subtle level: don't ingest things that aren't good for you, stay away from dangerous places, never tell a man named

> *The ideas I stand for*
> *are not mine.*
> *I borrowed them from Socrates.*
> *I swiped them from Chesterfield.*
> *I stole them from Jesus.*
> *And I put them in a book.*
> *If you don't like their rules,*
> *whose would you use?*
>
> DALE CARNEGIE

"Killer" his nose is crooked.

It continues on the mental and emotional levels: don't judge yourself or others, worry less, enough already with the guilts and resentments. There always seems to be a subtler level at which we can stop doing harm to ourselves and to others.

**2. Take care of yourself so you can help take care of others.** Physically: get enough (but not too much) food, enough water, enough exercise, enough rest. Mentally and emotionally: praise yourself for work well done, enjoy each moment, love yourself.

The second part of it, "so you can help take care of others," does not say you *must* help take care of others. It simply states the requirement ("take care of yourself") necessary for helping to take care of others *should you feel so inclined*. If you're not first taking care of yourself, you won't be able to help take care of others. If you don't take care of yourself, in fact, others will eventually be taking care of you.

**3. Use everything for your upliftment, learning, and growth.** *Everything*. No matter what you do, no matter how stupid, dumb, or damaging you judge it to be, there is a lesson to be learned from it. No matter what happens to you, no matter how unfair, inequitable, or wrong, there's something you can take from the situation and use for your upliftment, learning, or growth.

I'm not saying *intentionally* do silly things so you can learn from the inevitable disaster, or *solicit* evil so you can gain from it. We all do enough silly things and we have enough nastiness done unto us without having to create or invite more.

Remember the Writer's Creed: When the world gives you lemons, write *The Lemon Cookbook*.

There. Those three should keep you busy for, oh, the rest of your life. Explaining the many facets of these rules—and ways you can grow from them—will take me (at least) the remainder of this book.

*Look, I really don't
want to wax philosophic,
but I will say that if you're alive,
you got to flap your arms and legs,
you got to jump around a lot,
you got to make a lot of noise,
because life is the very opposite of death.
And therefore, as I see it,
if you're quiet, you're not living.
You've got to be noisy,
or at least your thoughts should
be noisy and colorful and lively.*

MEL BROOKS

# Participation

One of the greatest—and simplest—tools for learning more and growing more is *doing* more. It may or may not involve more activity. I'm not talking, necessarily, about action but of *involvement*.

When we're involved, we learn more. If you want to learn more, become an eager participant. Take part. Get involved. Plunge in. Embrace new experiences. Partake of life.

It's hard to recommend specific activities; what truly engages one person might be boredom personified to another. The cliché, of course, is to recommend taking a walk over watching television. But with the video revolution—122 channels of cable, video rentals, and all the rest—television can now be as involving as anything else.

It's not so much *what* you do, but how you *respond* to what you do. Does the activity involve you in an active way? Does it engage your mind, body, or emotions? (The full engagement of any *one* of these is participation.) Does it challenge you? Does it make you want to do more? If so, you're participating.

"Experimentation is an active science," Claude Bernard pointed out. Experiment. Make your life an active science.

> *The last of
> the human freedoms—
> to choose one's attitude
> in any given
> set of circumstances,
> to choose one's own way.*
>
> VIKTOR FRANKL

# Taking Charge

There's a lot of talk in personal growth circles about "taking charge." I often hear people exclaiming, "I'm going to take charge of that!" "Why aren't you taking charge of this?" "I'm taking charge of my life!"

Taking charge is great, but many people misunderstand what it is, exactly, they can take charge of.

As far as I can tell, the only thing you can take charge of is *the space within your skin*. That's it. Everything (and, especially, everyone) else does not belong to what you can take charge of.

Considering the vastness of the Universe, "the space within your skin" doesn't sound like much. But consider what's in there: your mind, your body, your emotions, and whatever sense of You you've got. That, to paraphrase Sir Thomas More, is not a bad public.

Even if we *could* take charge of people, things, and events outside ourselves, our first job would *still* be to take charge of ourselves.

What would "taking charge" be like?

You would have charge of your thoughts. You would not find yourself thinking about things you didn't want to think about. Your mind would be directed, creative, and positive at all times.

You would have charge of your body. You would be healthy, energetic, fit, glowing, radiant, exuberant, and fully alive.

You would have charge of your emotions. You

> *I'm not*
> *a very good*
> *advertisement*
> *for the American*
> *school system.*
>
> DAVID BRINKLEY

would never feel anything you didn't want to feel. You would feel joy, happiness, fulfillment, contentment, enthusiasm, or love whenever you wanted to.

To the degree we do not have charge of our minds, bodies, and emotions, we have our work cut out for us. Do we really have any *extra* time to spend taking charge of *others?*

*I was thrown out of NYU*
*for cheating*
*—with the dean's wife.*

WOODY ALLEN

*Computers are useless.*
*They can only*
*give you answers.*

PABLO PICASSO

# Open the Mind,
# Strengthen the Body,
# Fortify the Emotions

We often let one of The Big Three run the show. What I said earlier of the mind is equally true of the body and emotions—they make great servants, but bad masters.

You probably already know which of The Big Three you identify with most closely; the one you give most influence, the one that most often "leads you into temptation," the one that stops you from doing the things you really want to do—or know it would be best for you to do.

If you let *you* run the show, you'll probably learn more, and, even if you don't, the show will be a lot more enjoyable. (Wouldn't *you* rather choose which videos to watch?) Certainly *listen* to the advice of the mind, body, and emotions, but *you* make the choice, and move in the direction *you* choose. How? Here are some suggestions.

**Open the Mind.** We've probably all met our fair share of Descarteses running around, the ones who think therefore they am. You may have wanted to tell them, as Zorba told his "mental" young friend, "You think too much, that is your trouble. Clever people and grocers, they *weigh* everything."

These people spend a lot of time in opinions, evaluations, assessments, criticisms, judgments, convictions, laws, rules, procedures, schemes, and

> *You are a member*
> *of the British royal family.*
> *We are <u>never</u> tired,*
> *and we all <u>love</u> hospitals.*
>
> QUEEN MARY

making up their minds. Once their mind is made up, however, that's it; there's not much that can change it.

To these folk, one and all, I simply suggest: the mind is like a parachute; it works best when open. The mental amongst us may protest, "California bumper sticker philosophy!" All right, how about this thought from Henry James: "Always keep a window in the attic open; not just cracked: open."

**Strengthen the Body.** If you're not doing what you want because you're "too tired," or you're worried that some person, germ, or unlucky twist of fate is waiting to do you in, your body's probably got a hold of you.

Some people have a long list of physical reasons why they can't get things done: colds, flus, headaches, pulled this, sprained that, fractured something else. Is that what's troubling you, boobie?

Time to get hold of your body. Get up, get moving, get going. Your body is your vehicle, like your car. If you don't give your body direction, it's about as silly as letting your car choose its own direction. Get it out of the garage, step on the gas, get going.

It's your body: use it or lose it. Providing you give it sufficient rest, your body thrives on activity. Don't let your body stop you from doing what you want. Get up and do it anyway.

Don't wait for the energy before you do something; do and the energy will follow.

**Fortify the Emotions.** The overly emotional tend to wear their hearts on their sleeves. They act (or, more often, fail to act) because of what they feel. And what do they usually feel? Fear ("What if..."), guilt ("If I don't, then..."), anger ("You didn't..."), and disappointment ("Let down, as usual." [*Sings*] "Alone again, naturally").

These people stay away from events in which their emotions *might* be aroused—particularly the emotions of fear, guilt, anger, and disappointment ("hurt feelings"). They *fear* fear, guilt, anger, and disappointment, so they stay away.

To these dear hearts I say: persevere. Press on. Feel the fear and do it anyway. Although the phrase "scared to death" is often used by the emotionals, very few people have actually died from fear. Emo-

> *If you do not wish to be prone to anger, do not feed the habit; give it nothing which may tend to its increase. At first, keep quiet and count the days when you were not angry: "I used to be angry every day, then every other day: next, every two, then every three days!" and if you succeed in passing thirty days, sacrifice to the gods in thanksgiving.*
>
> EPICTETUS

tions are not fragile. They are there to be used.

You strengthen your influence over your emotions by using them. Consciously put yourself in situations you want to avoid because of your feelings. Feel all there is to feel and, later, remind yourself that you survived.

After a while, you'll do more than survive: you'll thrive. Because the other side of fear is excitement. And the other side of doing is the reward of achievement, which leads to the positive feelings you seek.

On the other hand, those who tend to be too often too angry at others need to exercise their feelings *less*. When we *don't* exercise something, it grows weaker. If you tend to lean toward resentment when things don't go your way, the next time you're peeved, try this: Rather than exercising your emotions, exercise your body. Run around the block. Do jumping jacks. Put on some music and dance. This may look silly to your friends and/or co-workers, but they'll probably prefer your taking a brief exercise break over the yelling, screaming, and/or pouting so often done by the easily ticked off.

(More on how to "take charge" of the mind, body, and emotions later.)

≈

Did any of these descriptions sound too close for comfort? At some point or other, we all tend to be too mental or too *un*physical or too emotional. If you've narrowed your specializations down to two and are having trouble choosing between them, maybe you have combined loyalties. This is not uncommon.

Some people, for example, are controlled by a combination of body and emotions. They add emotions to the usual lethargy of the body. These people are often hypochondriacs—and they have all the symptoms to prove it.

Some combine the body with the mind. These people may belong to The Flat Earth Society. They don't do much, and they know precisely *why* they shouldn't. These people would do well to exercise more, both mentally and physically—work cross-

> *What we have to do is to be*
> *forever curiously testing*
> *new opinions and*
> *courting new impressions.*

WALTER PATER

1873

word puzzles while jogging, for example.

Most common, it seems, are those who combine mind and emotions. When mind and emotions combine, it forms what is commonly referred to as "ego"—not necessarily by Freud's clinical definition, but by the more popular usage, as in "He has an ego problem," or "Her ego's out of control." The mind and emotions are a powerful combination. Learning to direct them only toward good— your own and others'—is a challenge of epic proportions, of epic achievements, and of epic rewards.

A great book is Dr. Albert Ellis's *How to Stubbornly Refuse to Make Yourself Miserable About Any-*

> *Practically all human misery*
> *and serious emotional turmoil*
> *are quite unnecessary*
> *—not to mention unethical.*
> *You, unethical?*
> *When you make yourself severely*
> *anxious or depressed,*
> *you are clearly acting against <u>you</u>*
> *and are being unfair and unjust*
> *to <u>yourself</u>.*

DR. ALBERT ELLIS

*thing—Yes, Anything!* Available from Institute for Rational-Emotive Therapy, 45 East 65th Street, New York, New York, 10021.

*There are seasons,*
*in human affairs,*
*when new depths seem to be*
*broken up in the soul,*
*when new wants*
*are unfolded in multitudes,*
*and a new and undefined good*
*is thirsted for.*
*There are periods when to dare,*
*is the highest wisdom.*

WILLIAM ELLERY CHANNING

1829

# Try New Things

The more we do, the more we learn. Even if we don't do it "right," we have at least learned another way of *not* doing it. That's learning; that's growth.

So, you don't (yet) know how to do something. So? "For the things we have to learn before we can do them," said Aristotle, "we learn by doing them."

I'm not suggesting you do more of what you already find comfortable. I'm encouraging you to explore the things you find *un*comfortable—the ones you're afraid to do, the ones you don't think you'd have the energy to do, the ones you're sure you'll be judged harshly by others if you do.

The underlying question in trying new things: Would I hurt myself *physically* (not emotionally, not mentally) if I did this? Not *could* (we *could* hurt ourselves doing almost anything), but *would*. If the answer is no, then do it.

It may not be comfortable (it's not supposed to be), and you may make a lot of mistakes (count on it), but you'll learn more than if you sat home in "That indolent but agreeable condition of doing nothing," as Pliny (the Younger) put it.

*And that's the way it is.*

WALTER CRONKITE

# Acceptance

Acceptance is such an important commodity, some have called it "the first law of personal growth."

Acceptance is simply seeing something the way it is and saying, "That's the way it is."

Acceptance is not approval, consent, permission, authorization, sanction, concurrence, agreement, compliance, sympathy, endorsement, confirmation, support, ratification, assistance, advocating, backing, maintaining, authenticating, reinforcing, cultivating, encouraging, furthering, promoting, aiding, abetting, or even *liking* what is.

Acceptance is saying, "It is what it is, and what is is what is." Philosophers from Gertrude Stein ("A rose is a rose is a rose") to Popeye ("I am what I am") have understood acceptance.

Until we truly accept *everything*, we can not see clearly. We will always be looking through the filters of "must's," "should's," "ought-to's," "have-to's," and prejudices.

When reality confronts our notion of what reality *should* be, reality always wins. (Drop something while believing gravity *shouldn't* make it fall. It falls anyway.) We don't like this (that is, we have trouble *accepting* this), so we either struggle with reality and become upset, or turn away from it and become unconscious. If you find yourself upset or unconscious—or alternating between the two—about something, you might ask yourself, "What am I not

> *Education is the ability
> to listen to almost anything
> without losing your temper
> or your self-confidence.*
>
> ROBERT FROST

accepting?"

Acceptance is not a state of passivity or inaction. I am not saying you can't change the world, right wrongs, or replace evil with good. Acceptance is, in fact, the first step to successful action. If you don't fully accept a situation precisely the way it is, you will have difficulty changing it. Moreover, if you don't fully accept the situation, you will never really know if the situation *should* be changed.

When you accept, you relax; you let go; you become patient. This is an enjoyable (and effective) place for either participation or departure. To stay and struggle (even for fun things: how many times have you tried *really hard* to have a good time?), or to run away in disgust and/or fear is not the most fulfilling way to live. One or the other, however, is the inevitable result of nonacceptance.

Take a few moments and consider a situation you are not happy with—not your greatest burden in life, just a simple event about which you feel peeved. Now accept *everything* about the situation. Let it be the way it is. Because, after all, it *is* that way, is it not? Also, if you accept it, you will feel better about it.

After accepting it, and everything about it, you probably still won't *like* it, but you may stop hating and/or fearing it. At least you will hate it or fear it a little less.

That's the true value of acceptance: you feel better about life, and about yourself. Everything I've said about acceptance also applies to things you have done (or failed to do). In fact, everything I've said about acceptance applies *especially* to your judgments of you.

All the things you think you should have done, and all the things you think you shouldn't have done, accept them. You did (or didn't) do them. That's reality. That's what happened. No changing the past. You can struggle with the past or pretend it didn't happen or you can accept it. I suggest the latter.

Even a prime-time disciplinarian such as Paul admitted,

> For what I do is not the good I want to do;
> no, the evil I do not want to do—this I keep

> *When you make a mistake,*
> *admit it.*
> *If you don't,*
> *you only*
> *make matters worse.*
>
> WARD CLEAVER

on doing. (Romans 7:19)

And *that* was a man who knew his should's. The next time you find yourself doing something you "shouldn't," or not doing something you "should," you might as well accept it. "If it was good enough for Paul, it's good enough for me."

While you're at it, you might as well accept all your future transgressions against the "should's," "must's," and "have-to's." You will transgress. Not that I necessarily *endorse* transgression—I simply accept the fact that human beings do *do* such things. Accept your humanity—with all the magnificence and folly inherent in it.

When you're in a state of nonacceptance, it's

difficult to learn. A clenched fist cannot receive a gift, and a clenched psyche—grasped tightly against the reality of what *must not be* accepted—cannot easily receive a lesson.

Relax. Accept what's already taken place—whether done by you or something outside of you. Then look for the lesson. You might not enjoy everything that happens in life, but you can enjoy the fact that no matter what happens, "there's a lesson in here someplace."

And don't forget: It's mostly genetic.

*I bid him look into*
*the lives of men*
*as though into a mirror,*
*and from others to take*
*an example for himself.*

TERENCE

190–159 B.C.

# The Mirror

When we look outside ourselves, we tend to evaluate. These evaluations tell us about the people and things around us.

These evaluations also tell us about *ourselves.*

Whatever we find "true" about the people and things around us, is also true about ourselves. When we evaluate anything outside ourselves, what we are doing is looking into a mirror; the mirror reflects back to us information about ourselves.

You may not always *like* what you see in the mirror; you may not always be comfortable with it; but, if you want to learn about yourself more quickly (and that's what the techniques in this section of the book will help you do), looking at yourself in the mirror of people and things is a valuable tool.

Remember the first time you heard your voice on a tape recorder, or saw yourself on videotape? "I don't sound like that!" "I don't behave that way!" Meanwhile, all your friends are saying, "Yes, that's what you sound like. Yes, that's precisely how you behave."

The first time *I* saw myself on videotape, I wondered how I had any friends at all. In time, with repeated viewings, I learned to accept the images of myself on the tape, and from that point of acceptance, I could begin making changes. (I like to think of them as *improvements.)*

> *When we see men*
> *of a contrary character,*
> *we should turn inwards*
> *and examine ourselves.*
>
> CONFUCIUS

And so it is with the mirror of life. You may not like all you see in the mirror, but until you look into the mirror and accept all that you see *about yourself,* you will not be able to make the changes (improvements) you'd like.

Let's say you look at someone and think, "She is angry, and I don't like that." Could it be you don't like being angry? If you look at someone and say, "He's scared to act. I wish he'd just *do it.*" Could there be something you're scared about; something you wish you would "just do"?

To evaluate and blame others does little good. What do we learn? That we can evaluate and blame? We probably already know we can do that.

Using the mirror, we see that we judge and blame *ourselves*. This is information we can do something about. We can, for example, stop judging and blaming ourselves, or accept the fact that we do judge and blame ourselves.*

Sometimes, we have to shift our focus a bit to see what it is about ourselves that's being reflected by others. For example, you may look at someone smoking and not like it. If you looked in that mirror, you might say, "I don't smoke, how does that apply to me?"

What is it you don't like about the other person's smoking? "It's unhealthy." Then, the question is: What do *you* do that's not healthy? "Smoking is inconsiderate." What do *you* do that's inconsiderate? "Smoking is a bad habit." What's your worst habit? "It's a waste of money." How do *you* waste money? "It shows no self-control." Where would you like more self-control?

Get the idea? There are other people's actions, and then there are the judgments we place on those actions. If we move from the *action* we judge, and look at the *judgment*, we usually find a similar judg-

---

*Most people, when they discover they judge and blame themselves, begin to judge and blame the fact that they judge and blame themselves. When they notice that they are judging and blaming themselves for judging and blaming themselves, they begin to judge and blame themselves for judging and blaming themselves for judging and blaming themselves. And some call it "personal growth."

> *It is no use to blame*
> *the looking glass*
> *if your face is awry.*
>
> NIKOLAI GOGOL
>
> 1836

ment we make about ourselves.

It's fun to extend this idea beyond people and include things: "This car never works when I want it to." What about you never works when you want it to? "It always rains at the worst possible time." What do you do at the worst possible time? "This steak is too tough." What about you could use a little tenderizing?

The mirror gives you lots of material on which to practice acceptance. You can learn to accept everything you already know about yourself, as well as everything you learn by looking into the mirror of other people's behavior. Your harshest judgments of others are the very ones that will benefit you most if you accept them about yourself.

The mirror also focuses you back on something (that is, *someone*) you *can* do something about. (Ever notice how little effect your judgments have on others?) Which brings us to our first Pop Quiz.

**To continually have "good advice" for a world that, for the most part, is completely disinterested in (and sometimes hostile to) advice of any kind:**

(A) is a waste of time

(B) is a waste of good advice

(C) tends to alienate self from others

(D) tends to alienate others from self

(E) promotes self-righteousness in the giver

(F) promotes resentment in the receiver

(G) all of the above

Guess who could *really use* all that good advice? For the answer, I quote from Michael Jackson's song "Man in the Mirror": "If you want to make the world a better place, take a look at yourself and make a change." All that good advice you've been giving to others (or would gladly give them if they only had the intelligence to ask) *finally* has a home. You.

And, as you're the only one you can really change, the only one who can really use all your good advice is you. Isn't it wonderful that the *advice giver* and the *best user* of the advice are the same person? (If you're thinking, "I have to tell so-and-so this. She needs to take some more of her own ad-

> *Why do you look at the speck of sawdust*
> *in your brother's eye*
> *and pay no attention*
> *to the plank in your own eye?*
> *How can you say to your brother,*
> *"Let me take the speck out of your eye,"*
> *when all the time there is*
> *a plank in your own eye?*
> *You hypocrite,*
> *first take the plank out of your own eye,*
> *and then you will*
> *see clearly to remove the speck*
> *from your brother's eye.*
>
> JESUS OF NAZARETH

vice," remember the mirror. It's probably *you* who needs to take more of *your own* advice.)

Again, sometimes we must shift the focus and ask ourselves the larger question in order to see how the advice we give another would fit ourselves.

If your advice to someone is to be more careful with his money, and you don't need that advice, what *do* you need to be more careful about? If your advice to another is to exercise more, and you already exercise a lot, what part of yourself (other than your body) could do with a bit more exercise?

When we look into the mirror of life and see all there is within ourselves that needs improvement, we know we're going to be at it for some time:

changing what we can, doing our best with what we can't, accepting and forgiving it all—whenever we remember to do so. (I know, for example, that I'm really writing this book for myself, and if you care to look over my shoulder as I learn from my own "good advice," you are most welcome.)

We also see that whenever we lash out at another, we are really lashing out at ourselves. In this context, to strike another is as silly as striking the bathroom mirror because it's giving us a reflection we don't like. We can only pray that in our striking out, we don't hurt the mirror (especially when that mirror is another person). Could that be where the superstition, "If you break a mirror, it's seven years bad luck," comes from?

Thus far, I've only been talking about the "glass darkly" side of the mirror concept. It does have a lighter side—mirrors also reflect what's good about us.

All the people and things that you find loving, affectionate, caring, devoted, tender, wonderful, compassionate, beautiful, adorable, magnificent, and sacred are simply mirroring to you the loving, affectionate, caring, devoted, tender, wonderful, compassionate, beautiful, adorable, magnificent, and sacred parts of yourself.

The lighter side of the mirror is sometimes more difficult for people to accept than the darker side. "I can see that I'm impatient when I judge someone else for being impatient," you may say, "but when I see the majesty of a mountain, what does that have to do with me?" Everything. That

> *Mirrors should reflect a little before throwing back images.*
>
> JEAN COCTEAU

purple mountain majesty is in you, too.

In fact, it's not really in the mountain at all. What's in the mountain is *rock*. What we, as humans, *project onto* the mountain is majesty. That's one of the reasons the mirror concept works. Most of the time we are projecting *something* onto almost *everything*. When the projection returns to us, we can see it as a reflection—which it is—or we can pretend it is emanating from the thing we projected the reflection onto.

The illusion that what we projected is coming from the thing we projected it onto is deceptive. We tend to get lost in the illusion, just as we tend to get lost in the illusion of images projected on a movie screen. It is, nonetheless, an illusion, and the source of the projection at the movie theater is the projector. The source of the things we think and feel about others is ourselves.

Using the mirror concept, we can begin to recognize the true source of the projections we send out. We begin to see that this person wasn't so bad after all. It was, in fact, what we were projecting onto him. We see that this other person wasn't so wonderful after all. We were merely projecting our wonderfulness upon her.

The more you use it, the more you will probably find the mirror concept works. This is an advanced tool for learning. There is, however, an *advanced* advanced version of this. It's called relationships.

*The best mirror*
*is an old friend.*

GEORGE HERBERT

1651

# Relationships

Most people seek relationships to *get away from themselves.* But not eager learners! We use everything for our upliftment, learning, and growth—including relationships.

Relationships can be among the most amazing mirrors around. Some relationships are like funhouse mirrors: they reflect an image back to you, but it's liable to be distorted. Other relationships are like magnifying or reducing mirrors: they make everything seem larger or smaller.

Some relationships are accurate mirrors of the darkness inside us; others accurately reflect the light. Occasionally, we find one that reflects both. That's the relationship we either flee from, or "grapple to our hearts with hoops of steel."

I'm using the term *relationship* in the broadest sense. Relationships truly take place inside ourselves. We have a relationship with anyone or anything we encounter. Have you ever read a book by an author you never met and still felt a relationship? Or felt close to a movie character, knowing the character never even existed?

What we do inside ourselves about the people (and things) we choose to be in relationship with can be one of the greatest learning tools we can use—especially when combined with the mirror. This lays the foundation for not just learning, but for enjoyable, productive relationships with others.

*What the inner voice says*
*Will not disappoint*
*the hoping soul.*

SCHILLER

1797

# Inner Voices

It doesn't take much inner listening to know that "in there" there are many voices: speaking, singing, shouting, and whispering. At times, I'm sure I have an entire Mormon Tabernacle Choir.

Some of the "voices" speak; others flash images. Some communicate by feelings, while others communicate through a sense of "knowing." When I say "voices," I include all of these—and any forms of communication I failed to mention.

These voices have information—all of it useful. Some you can use by acting on; some you can use by doing precisely the opposite. It's a matter of knowing whether or not a given voice is on your side.

How do you know? Listen. *Listen* might not be the best word. *Perceive* might be a better word, or *look within,* or *be aware of* your inner process. I'll use *listen,* because it goes along with the analogy of "voices," but know that when I say "listen" I also mean watch, sense, perceive, and be aware of what's going on inside.

Start by listening and keeping track of which voice says what. You can assign them characters, if you like. Here are four of my inner favorites:

**The critic.** I see this voice as a vulture. Pick, pick, pick, nag, nag, nag. Nothing anyone does is good enough. (Except occasionally when somebody else does something undeniably outstanding, then the vulture says, "Well, *you'll* never do anything *that*

> *I will neither yield*
> *to the song of the siren*
> *nor the voice of the hyena,*
> *the tears of the crocodile*
> *nor the howling of the wolf.*

GEORGE CHAPMAN

1605

good.") Doom and gloom fly with the vulture. It feeds on unworthiness, and its droppings are the doubts, fears, and judgments that keep us from moving toward our goals.

**The praiser.** The praiser I see as an eagle. It proudly tells us all the wonderful things we are, have, and do. It generously praises the being, accomplishments, and activities of others. It's the one that lets us know we are worthy *no matter what,* and that our worth does not need to be proven, earned, or defended. We are worthy just because we *are.* All that we are is fine just the way it is. It flies on the wings of grace and gratitude. It nurtures our very soul.

**The dummy.** The dummy is a turkey. It's the one who answers quickly and loudly, "I don't know," to almost any question. The turkey is the one that keeps us doing all those stupid things we do, and then say, "Darn! I knew better!" We may know better, but no one told the turkey. Turkeys do not fly. If you leave them out in the rain they will drown. They have nothing to be thankful for on Thanksgiving.

**The grower.** The grower is like an egg. An egg? Yes, as W. S. Gilbert said, "As innocent as a new-laid egg." That's one of the attributes of growth—each moment is new, fresh, and innocent. An egg also contains all the potential for future growth. As Hans Christian Andersen pointed out, "His own image was no longer the reflection of a clumsy, dirty, gray bird, ugly and offensive. He himself was a swan! Being born in a duck yard does not matter, if only you are hatched from a swan's egg." Our grower knows who we are and the kind of bird in the egg (HINT: It's no vulture). It has sufficient self-love to keep itself warm and cozy while gestating. It knows the hatching will take place at precisely the right moment. It is content and divinely patient until then. As Robert Burns wrote of his egg, "The voice of Nature loudly cries, / And many a message from the skies, / That something in us never dies."

It's a good idea to listen to *what* the voices say, not to *how* they say it. As Lord Byron reminds us, "The Devil hath not, / in all his quiver's choice, / An arrow for the heart like a sweet voice." And

> *The voice of the turtledove*
> *speaks out.*
> *It says:*
> *Day breaks,*
> *which way are you going?*
> *Lay off, little bird,*
> *must you so scold me?*
> *I found my lover on his bed,*
> *and my heart was sweet to excess.*
>
> LOVE SONGS OF THE NEW KINGDOM
>
> 1550–1080 B.C.

Freud, a century later, wrote, "The voice of the intellect is a soft one, but it does not rest until it has gained a hearing. Ultimately, after endlessly repeated rebuffs, it succeeds. This is one of the few points in which one may be optimistic about the future of mankind, but in itself it signifies not a little."

If all these birds in our brains are too much for you, perhaps you could use the metaphor of tuning a radio, or changing channels on a television. Once you tune into your own network of wisdom, you'll have guidance that's sure, clear, and direct.

*I thank you for your voices,*
*thank you,*
*Your most sweet voices.*

SHAKESPEARE

*More than any time
in history mankind
faces a crossroads.
One path leads to despair
and utter hopelessness,
the other to total extinction.
Let us pray that we have
the wisdom to choose correctly.*

WOODY ALLEN

# Accountability

To the degree the events of the world happen *to* us, we are powerless pawns in a game of chance. The most we can do is hope, have lots of insurance, and buy emergency food supplies.

To the degree we know that *we* have *something* to do with what happens to us, we gain authority, influence, and control over our lives. We see that by changing our attitudes and actions, we can change what happens to us.

In a word, we become accountable.

When something happens to you, you can explore it and probably see that you had *something* to do with its taking place. You either created it, promoted it, or—at the very least—*allowed* it. (To remember the words *create, promote* and *allow,* just remember C.P.A. = accountant = accountability.)

When looking for areas of accountability, please don't start with the biggest disaster of your life. Start with the daily slings and arrows that flesh is heir to. Looking for accountability is like exercise—don't try to run a marathon if, like me, you've been sedentary for twenty years (and supine the twenty years before that).

Pick a simple "it happened to me" event—misplacing your keys, the plumber not showing up, running out of gas—and see how you *might* have had *something* to do with creating, promoting, or allowing it to happen. Helpful hints:

**1. Go back in time.** We love to begin our "vic-

> *Well, if you've got*
> *work to do, Wallace,*
> *I don't want to interfere.*
> *I was reading an article*
> *in the paper the other day*
> *where a certain amount*
> *of responsibility around*
> *the home was good*
> *character training.*
> *Good-bye, Mr. and Mrs. Cleaver.*
>
> EDDIE HASKELL

tim stories" at the point "it" starts happening *to* us—when the you-know-what hits the fan, and the fan is running. If you start at an earlier point, however, you see that you promised yourself to always put your keys in the same place but didn't, the plumber was not known for his reliability, and the low-gas indicator light on your car had been on for so long you thought your car was solar-powered.

**2. What was I pretending not to know?** What intuitive flashes did you ignore? "I'd better get some spare keys made," as you passed the hardware store a month ago? "This guy's not going to show," when you first spoke to the plumber? "I'd better get some gas," as you passed the thirty-fifth station since the gas-indicator light came on? We all *pretend* to know less than we really know.

Into all this comes a perfectly good word that has been given a bad rap—*responsibility*. Responsibility simply means the *ability* to *respond*. Most people, however, use it to mean blame: "Who's responsible for this!"

In any situation, we have the ability to respond, and our response will make the situation either better or worse. Whichever way it goes, we have the ability to respond again. And again. And again. By exercising our ability to respond, and watching the results closely, we can, if we choose, lift almost any situation.

One ability to respond we always have is how we react *inside* to what's going on *outside*. The world can be falling apart around us; that doesn't mean we have to fall apart ourselves. It's okay to feel good when things go bad. (See the chapter "Taking Charge.")

True accountability has three parts. First, acknowledge that you have *something* to do with what's happened. Even if you're not sure what that might be, ask yourself, "How *might I* have created, promoted, or allowed this?" The answer may surprise you.

Second, explore your response options. In other words, become response-able.

Third, take a corrective action. The more accountability you found at the first step, the more corrective action you may want to take. On the

> *Honest criticism is hard to take,*
> *particularly from a relative,*
> *a friend, an acquaintance,*
> *or a stranger.*
>
> FRANKLIN P. JONES

other hand, your corrective action might be getting out of the way and letting those who are more accountable than you take care of things—if you spilt the glass of milk, clean up the milk; if a milk truck spills milk all over the highway, get off the highway.

And remember: you create, promote, or allow all the *good* things that happen to you, too.

*There is no human problem*
*which could not be solved*
*if people would simply*
*do as I advise.*

GORE VIDAL

When an emotional injury takes place,
the body begins
a process as natural as the
healing of a physical wound.
Let the process happen.
Trust that nature will do the healing.
Know that the pain will pass and,
when it passes,
you will be stronger, happier,
more sensitive and aware.

HOW TO SURVIVE THE LOSS OF A LOVE

# Good Mourning

This is a lifetime of good-byes. In our time, we will say good-bye to cherished people, things, and ideas. Eventually, we say good-bye to life itself with our death. Learn to say a good good-bye. Allow yourself to mourn each loss. As with a physical wound, the body has its own schedule for healing. It will tell you when it has healed.

Understanding the process of recovering from an emotional wound is valuable—not necessarily as a technique for accelerating the healing process—but more as an assurance that, no matter what stage of recovery you are in, all is well.

There are three distinct, yet overlapping, phases of recovery. We go through each phase no matter what the loss. The only difference is duration and intensity of feeling. In a minor loss, we can experience all three stages in a few minutes. In a major loss, the recovery process can take years.

The first stage is **shock/denial/numbness.** Our body and emotions numb themselves to the pain. The mind denies the loss. Often, the first words we utter after hearing of a loss are "Oh, no," or "This can't be."

The second stage is **fear/anger/depression**. We are angry at whatever or whoever caused the loss (including the person who left). We often turn the anger against ourselves and feel guilt over something we did or did not do. (This assignment of blame, either outer or inner, is not always ra-

> *In the darkest hour*
> *the soul is replenished*
> *and given strength*
> *to continue and endure.*
>
> HEART WARRIOR CHOSA

tional.) The depression stage of recovery is the sadness often associated with loss: the tears, the hurt, the desolation. We fear the pain will never end; that we will never love or be loved again.

The third stage is **understanding/acceptance/moving on.** We realize that life goes on, that loss is a part of life, and that our life can and will be complete without the presence of what was lost. We also realize, by going through the first two stages of recovery, we have learned a great deal about ourselves, and we are a better person for the experience.

If we don't allow ourselves the time to heal, some of our ability to experience life is frozen—

locked away—and is unavailable for the "up" experiences we enjoy: happiness, contentment, love. The part of us that feels the anger and depression is the same part that feels peace and love. If you refuse to feel the anger and the pain of a loss, you will not be able to feel anything else until that area heals.

In other words, stay out of your own way. Let yourself feel bad if you want to feel bad. Feel joy, too. Healing is taking place.

Give yourself the gift of healing.*

*You might want to read *How to Survive the Loss of a Love* (by Melba Colgrove, Ph.D., Harold Bloomfield, M.D., and me. Please call 1-800-LIFE-101).

*I don't want the cheese,*
*I just want*
*to get out of the trap.*

SPANISH PROVERB

# Learn to Let Go

How does one avoid loss in the first place? Contrary to popular belief, it's not *attachment* that causes loss—attachment feels fine. It's *de*tachment that hurts. Learn to let go.

Some suggest that to avoid loss, one should never be attached to anything. They give the example of a hand in water: when the hand is removed from the water, the hand leaves no impression. These people say the reason the hand leaves no trace in the water is because the water is not attached to the hand.

On the contrary, while the hand is in the water, it is *very* attached to the hand—surrounding, enfolding, and embracing it. Allow yourself to experience life as fully as water experiences the hand; then, as completely, let go.

Yes, the water leaves a little of itself on the departing hand, as we leave a little of ourselves with the people and things we touch. For the most part, however, when it comes time to go, let go.

The hand can no more hold the water than the water can hold the hand. As soon as one "wants" to leave, there is no attachment. Hand and water both accept the inevitability, and part "clean."

There is a title for a book on raising children I've always liked: *Hold Them Very Close, and Let Them Go.* This I find good advice for all experiences:

Hold them very close, and let them go.

*You do not need to leave your room.*
*Remain sitting at your table and listen.*
*Do not even listen,*
*simply wait.*
*Do not even wait,*
*be quite still and solitary.*
*The world will freely*
*offer itself to you*
*to be unmasked,*
*it has no choice,*
*it will roll in ecstasy at your feet.*

FRANZ KAFKA

# Observation

You might think of observation as a meditation of acceptance. You sit and simply accept *everything* that happens, both inner and outer. Consider: almost the only time you want to respond to something outside yourself is when something *inside* demands it.

What is that inner demand? What is the voice (or voices) that insists you do this, or run away from that? Why do you sometimes follow that voice automatically—maybe even unconsciously? The answers to these questions lie in observation.

To observe, don't *do* anything; simply notice the inner process. The voices demanding you do this, move there, or scratch whatever may rise to screaming crescendo. Don't do anything; continue to observe.

At first, observation is best practiced alone. Set a timer. Start with, say, five minutes and build up. Sit in a comfortable position, close your eyes, and tell yourself, "I'm not going to move my body until the timer goes off." Then sit and observe.

The inner voices may start quietly, but as they feel "ignored," they tend to get louder. One may want you to shift your position. Don't. Observe the voice demanding that you shift. One may want you to scratch an itch. Don't. Observe the itch; observe the emotional reaction to not scratching the itch. ("It's my body, and I can scratch it if I want to!") Observe it all. If the phone rings, observe the desire

> *If you resist evil,*
> *as soon as it's gone,*
> *you'll fold.*
>
> KEN KESEY

to answer it. Don't answer it. Observe it. Observe your inner reaction to an outer ringing.

Observation may sound easy on paper. The inner voices that don't want to lose control often say at this point, "That would be no problem for us; we don't need to do that exercise." Try it and see.

As we increase the amount of time we observe while sitting still, we can then start observing while moving around.

Time for a Pop Quiz!

**Observation shows us:**

(A) our inner reactions to outer experiences

(B) that it's our *reaction* to what happens

around us, not what happens around us, that motivates us

(C) the demands the voices inside us make

(D) that we don't have to do anything with, to, or about the voices

(E) that we don't have to do anything about most outer experiences

(F) all of the above

Observation leads us to a point of neutrality—a place where we don't *have to* react, either positively or negatively, to any situation. We simply *are.*

Neutrality is not neuter, nor is it like "Neutral" in a car. *We* can engage our gears and move ahead *and* remain neutral. In fact, when we're not reacting—almost reflexively—to this, that, and everything, our action becomes more effective. We can maintain an inner calm and still be dynamically involved.

Another way of viewing this: observation disconnects our "buttons." We know that when someone "pushes our button," we react. Push, react. Push, react. Push, react. We are no longer in control; the person or thing pushing the button is.

Through observation, we notice that it's not the *pushing* of the button, but our *reaction* to the pushing that causes our response. Eventually, by intentionally not responding and simply observing, we dissolve the push-react connection. (We will discuss in Parts Four and Five ways of reconnecting the buttons to the responses *you* want.)

Think of "observing" as "obviously serving"

> *Every man has one thing*
> *he can do better than anyone else*
> *and usually it is reading his own*
> *handwriting.*
>
> G. NORMAN COLLIE

yourself, and "neutral" as "new trails" of freedom, fun, and adventure.

*Trying to define yourself
is like trying to bite
your own teeth.*

ALAN WATTS

*I hear that you're building*
*Your house*
*deep in the desert.*
*Are you living for*
*nothing now?*
*I hope you're keeping*
*Some kind of record.*

LEONARD COHEN
"FAMOUS BLUE RAINCOAT"

# Keep a Record of Your Progress

Record each day, in some way

- The lessons you learn

- The good that you do

- The good that happens to you

- The insights you have

- Anything else that seems of importance or interest

The "classical" way of recording such things is, of course, a journal, or a diary. ("Keep a diary, and someday your diary will keep you."—Mae West.) Your record-keeping need not, however, be that formal. You might have a box into which you toss mementos, letters, matchbook covers (etc.), and dated notes to yourself.

In this electronic age, you might keep a file in your computer. Using your word processor, you can include copies of your best letters, poems, etc. in your journal file, and then use the best from your electronic journal in letters, manuscripts, and so on.

You could use a tape recorder and "debrief" yourself each evening, or take one along and record things "as they happen."

You could try a video log: sit in front of a video camera each day and talk about the previous

> *To be one's self,*
> *and unafraid whether right or wrong,*
> *is more admirable*
> *than the easy cowardice*
> *of surrender to conformity.*
>
> IRVING WALLACE

twenty-four hours, or record a voice-over as the camera explores the physical memorabilia of the day.

The key here, as with all my suggestions (and, for that matter, life itself), is flexibility and fun.

A second key: do whatever you'll *consistently do*. Don't start an Epic Production that will be abandoned in a short while (with the best intentions of returning to it, of course). Build up to that. For now, you might start by scribbling a note or two in the margins of this book as you go along.

*Creativity is a drug*
*I cannot live without.*

CECIL B. deMILLE

*I'm going to
turn on the light,
and we'll be two people
in a room
looking at each other
and wondering
why on earth we were
afraid of the dark.*

GALE WILHELM

# Light

If you've used the light before, you know whether or not it works for you. This will be a reminder. If you've never used light, then consider this chapter the parameters of an experiment. Please neither believe nor disbelieve that this tool is effective; simply try it in a variety of situations, and see what happens.

Using the light is very easy. You simply ask that the light (you can imagine it as a clear, pure white light) be sent somewhere for the highest good of all concerned. That's it. That's using the light.

In fact, light can't be "sent"—it's all around all the time everywhere anyway. In a sense, it's as silly to "send" light as it is to "send" air. (When I was traveling in Israel, however, I did buy a can of "Air From the Holy Land.") We do ask the light that's already there (or here) to "do its thing" for the highest good.

How do we know the light "worked"? Sometimes the situation changes, sometimes our attitude about the situation changes, and sometimes both.

Things may not change the way we *want* them to change. The light is not a bellhop in the sky. It will not do what you want at the expense of others—or yourself. As Oscar Wilde pointed out, "When the gods choose to punish us, they merely answer our prayers." To have *all* of our desires fulfilled would be a curse.

That's where the "highest good" comes in. We

> *Man is his own star,*
> *and the soul that can*
> *Render an honest and a*
> *perfect man*
> *Commands all light,*
> *all influence, all fate.*

JOHN FLETCHER

1647

don't always know what the highest good is. (We often *think* we do or *feel* we do—but haven't our thoughts and feelings been wrong in the past?) That's why I suggest that, when you use the light, you add "...for the highest good of all concerned." The "highest good" is the safety clause. We don't want to play Sorcerer's Apprentice with our—or others'—lives.

Using the light doesn't require an elaborate ritual or procedure. It takes almost no time. You can get it down to three words: "light, highest good." If you're concerned about someone or something, add "light, highest good" to the concern, and let it go. Then, if you so choose, *do something* about improving the situation. If you choose not to get physically involved, send the light and let it go. You've done all that you can do, which, you may find, is quite a lot.

In what situations can you use the light? In what situations can you use air? I can't imagine a situation in which you *couldn't* use the light. Just before dropping off to sleep, some people ask for the light to surround, fill, protect, bless, and heal them, for their highest good and the highest good of all concerned. When they wake up, they ask the light not only to be with them, but also to go ahead of them, preparing the day for their highest good.

Using light is not a religion, any more than using air is a religion. People who claim light as an exclusive part of their doctrine might as well claim that only its believers can enjoy the benefits of air. The light can be used as an adjunct to any religious or spiritual path you are on, or it can be used in a purely secular way.

Eventually, using the light becomes as automatic as breathing.

*See golden days,*
*fruitful of golden deeds,*
*With Joy and Love*
*triumphing.*

JOHN MILTON

1667

# Visualization

In a sense, it's unfortunate the term *visualization* has become the almost-exclusive word for any work done using the imagination. The word *visual* is, of course, connected to sight. People try a moment or two of *"visualization,"* say they never "saw" anything, and give up. When they hear about the wonders of visualization, they assume it's another one of "those things" that other people can do, but they can't.

Actually, a great many people never "see" a thing during visualization. Others have murky images. Some only have a "sense" or feeling of things. Others hear the "images." Few people, in fact, see the crisp, clear, Technicolor images we assume most everybody (but us) sees.

We all "visualize." If I asked you to draw a circle, you could do it. A circle is a visual thing. You had to "envision" it. However you "saw" the circle in your imagination, that's how you'll "see" while visualizing.

Don't remember how you "saw" the circle? Try a triangle. How about a square? "It's just *there*," you might say. Or maybe you notice, "It takes a little while, but then it appears." Either one is fine.

Now graduate school. Think of the Eiffel Tower. The Statue of Liberty. The moon. An orange. A lemon. A lake. A rose. What color is the rose? Is it a red, red rose, or are you from Texas? Some get an "image" instantly, others take as long

> *The real distinction is between those*
> *who adapt their purposes to reality*
> *and those who seek to mould reality*
> *in the light of their purposes.*
>
> HENRY KISSINGER

as five seconds each. (And five seconds can seem like a long time.) However you got these—be it a sense, feeling, verbal description, or an image— that's how you visualize.

Most of us spend a great deal of time believing *visual lies*. We have an image of our unworthiness, believe it, and that gives birth to one imagined failure after another. The unworthiness is a lie, but the projected failures can come true: what we focus on, we can become.

With visualization, you begin to tell yourself visual truths.

*There is only one admirable*
*form of the imagination:*
*the imagination that is so intense*
*that it creates a new reality,*
*that it makes things happen,*
*whether it be a political thing*
*or a social thing*
*or a work of art.*

SEAN O'FAOLAIN

*I discovered the
"something"
in
"nothing."*

BARBRA STREISAND

# The Sanctuary

A sanctuary is an inner retreat you build with visualization in your imagination. Here you can discover the truth about yourself, and work to affirm it. ("Make it firm.")

I call it a sanctuary. Some call it a workshop, or an inner classroom. You can call it whatever word gives you the sense of asylum, harbor, haven, oasis, shelter—a place you can go to learn your lessons in peace and harmony, or just take a rest and get away from it all.

There are absolutely no limits to your sanctuary, although it's a good idea to put *some* limits on it. In this way, the sanctuary is a transitional point between the limitations of our physical existence and the unlimited.

The sanctuary can be any size, shape, or dimension you choose—large and elaborate or small and cozy. It can be located anywhere—floating in space, on a mountain top, by an ocean, in a valley, anywhere. (You are welcome to combine all these, if you like.) The nice thing about the sanctuary: you can change it or move it anytime—instantly.

The sanctuary can contain anything. I'll suggest some things here, but consider this just the beginning of your shopping list. Before giving my design tips (you can consider me your *interior* designer), I'll talk about ways in which you might want to "build" your sanctuary.

Some people will build theirs by simply reading

> *The doctor can bury his mistakes*
> *but an architect can only advise*
> *his client to plant vines.*

FRANK LLOYD WRIGHT

the suggestions: as they read each, it's there. Others might read them over now for information, and then put on some soft music, close their eyes, and let the construction begin. Still others may want to make this an *active* process. With their eyes closed (and being careful not to bump into too much furniture), they might physically move as each area of the sanctuary is built. Any—or any combination—of these is, of course, fine.

While reading through my suggestions, you will probably get ideas for additions or alterations. By all means make notes of these, or simply incorporate them as you go. Have I gotten across the idea that this is *your* sanctuary? Okay, let's go.

**Entryway.** This is a door or some device that responds only to you and lets only you enter. (I'll suggest a way to bring others into your sanctuary in a moment.)

**Light.** Each time you enter your sanctuary, a pure, white light cascades over you, surrounding, filling, protecting, blessing, and healing you—for your highest good, and the highest good of all concerned.

**Main Room.** Like the living room of a house or the lobby of a hotel, this is the central area. From here, there are many directions you can go and many things to explore.

**People Mover.** This is a device to move people in and out of your sanctuary. No one ever enters without your express permission and invitation. You can use an elevator, conveyor belt, *Star Trek* beam-me-up device, or anything else that moves people. Let there be a white light at the entry of the mover as well, so that as people enter and leave your sanctuary, they are automatically surrounded, filled, protected, and healed by that white light, and only that which is for their highest good and the highest good of all concerned takes place.

**Information Retrieval System.** This is a method of getting any kind of information—providing, of course, it's for your highest good (and the highest good of all concerned) that you have it. The information retrieval system can be a computer screen, a staff of librarians, a telephone, or any other device that will answer your questions.

**Video Screen.** This is a video (or movie) screen

> *If you have built*
> *castles in the air,*
> *your work need not be lost;*
> *that is where they should be.*
>
> *Now put the foundations*
> *under them.*
>
> HENRY DAVID THOREAU

on which you can view various parts of your life—past, present, or future. The screen has a white light around it. When you see images you don't like or don't want to encourage, the light is off. When the screen displays images you want to affirm, the light glows. (Those who are old enough to remember Sylvania's Halo of Light television know just what I mean.)

**Ability Suits.** This is a closet of costumes that, when worn, give you the instant ability to be anything you want—great actor, successful writer, perfect lover, eager learner, Master of your Universe; any and all are available to you. When you're done with an ability suit, just throw it on the floor in front of the closet—ability suits have the ability to hang themselves up.

**Ability Suit Practice Area.** This is a place you can try new skills—or improve on old ones—while wearing your ability suits. Leave lots of room, because there's an ability suit for flying and another for space travel. In your sanctuary, not even the sky's a limit.

**Health Center.** Here the healing arts of all the ages—past, present, future; traditional and alternative—are gathered in one place. All are devoted to your greater health. The health center is staffed with the most competent health practitioners visualization can buy. Who is the most healing being you can imagine? That's who runs your center.

**Playroom.** Here, all the toys you ever wanted —as a child or as an adult—are gathered. There's lots of room—and time—to play with each. As with ability suits, you never have to worry about "putting your toys away." They put themselves away.

**Sacred Room.** This is a special sanctuary within your sanctuary. You can go there for meditation, contemplation, or special inner work.

**Master Teacher.** This is your ideal teacher, the being with whom you are the perfect student. The Master Teacher knows everything about you (has always been with you, in fact). The Master Teacher also knows all you need to learn, the perfect timing for your learning it, and the ideal way of teaching it to you. You don't *create* a Master Teacher—that's already been done. You *discover* your Master

> *Imagination*
> *is more important*
> *than knowledge.*
>
> ALBERT EINSTEIN

Teacher. To meet your Master Teacher, simply walk over to your people mover, ask for your Master Teacher to come forth, and from the pure, white light of your people mover comes your Master Teacher.

(I'll leave you two alone for a while. More uses for the sanctuary later. See you both in Part Three!)

*Everyone is necessarily*
*the hero of his own life story.*

JOHN BARTH

*A problem is a chance*
*for you to do your best.*

DUKE ELLINGTON

# PART THREE

## MASTER TEACHERS
## IN DISGUISE

Your Master Teacher—as wonderful as your Master Teacher is—is not the only Master Teacher in your life. Far from it.

Most people think Master Teachers are only "in the skies." Not so. They're here, there, and everywhere. Why don't we recognize them as such? Because they are also masters of disguise.

How do they disguise themselves? Only as some of the most potentially powerful learning tools in our lives: mistakes, guilt and resentment, fear, pain and disease, stubbornness, addictions, depression, death, emergencies—all the things most people would, if they could, eliminate.

Some try awfully hard to eliminate them, too. Ever notice the themes of many bestselling self-help books? How to get rid of this Master Teacher, how to dispose of that Master Teacher, 101 ways to eradicate some other Master Teacher.

Why would we not take advantage of potential sources of wisdom in our lives? Maybe we forgot that they are teachers—or maybe nobody ever explained it to us.

> *Shall I crack any*
> *of those old jokes, master,*
> *At which the audience*
> *never fail to laugh?*

ARISTOPHANES

405 B.C.

Let's pretend your Master Teachers sent me here to explain what they have to offer you and what great friends they are. That way maybe you'll use them and stop giving them such a bad name. Consider me the goodwill ambassador for Master Teachers in Disguise Guild.

There is a funny scene from the musical *Showboat*. Two mountain men, who have never seen a play, stumble into the showboat theater, unaware that the actors are acting in a play. They converse with the heroine and encourage the hero. When the villain arrives, they chase him off the stage with six-guns. The mountaineers are proud of themselves for having done "the right thing."

The irony in this, of course, is that the audience, watching *Showboat*, forgets the men playing the mountaineers are actors, too. The audience laughs at the naiveté of people mistaking play-acting for real-life. In order to appreciate the humor, however, the audience watching *Showboat* must be lost in the illusion themselves.

That's how the Master Teachers get away with the disguise: we forget they are sources of wisdom—and seldom are we interested in remembering again. If someone stood up during a performance of *Showboat* and began yelling, "Those aren't mountain men! Those are actors! Those aren't real guns! Those are props!" the person would be ushered from the theater.

The Master Teachers need the same illusion to teach as well as they do. The more we believe the characters in a movie (and forget they're really actors), the more moving the movie can be. Thus, the more we believe the Master's disguise, the more powerful and complete the lesson.

So why am I spilling the beans?

If you're struggling too much with the teacher, you might not stand back and learn the lesson. The techniques in this section of the book allow you to take that step back. You can learn from past Master Teaching sessions—all that you might have considered the doom and gloom of your past. You can also use the techniques to learn more quickly the ongoing lessons being taught by your Master Teachers.

But by exposing the Master Teachers (the "vil-

> *Good behavior*
> *is the last refuge*
> *of mediocrity.*
>
> HENRY S. HASKINS

lains" of the piece) as the wonderful, kindly, loving friends they are, am I not risking the effectiveness of future lessons?

Not likely.

You'll forget all this.

*You're obviously suffering*
*from delusions of adequacy.*

ALEXIS CARRINGTON

DYNASTY

*Experience is the name
everyone gives
to their mistakes.*

Oscar Wilde

# Mistakes

One of the least disguised of the Master Teachers in Disguise is mistakes. Mistakes, obviously, show us what needs improving. Without mistakes, how would we know what we had to work on?

This process seems an invaluable aid to learning, and yet many people avoid situations in which they might make mistakes. Many people also deny or defend the mistakes they've made—or may be making.

There is a story told of Edison, who made, say, 1,000 unsuccessful attempts before arriving at the lightbulb. "How did it feel to fail 1,000 times?" a reporter asked. "I didn't fail 1,000 times," Edison replied. "The lightbulb was an invention with 1,001 steps."

Why don't most of us see our own lives in this way? I think it goes back to unworthiness. We assume a façade of perfection in a futile attempt to *prove* our worthiness. "An unworthy person couldn't be this perfect," the façade maintains. Alas, being human, we make mistakes. Mistakes crack the façade. As the façade crumbles, a frantic attempt is made to hide the hideous thing (unworthiness) the façade was designed to hide—from ourselves as much as from others.

If we didn't play this game of denial with ourselves, we would make mistakes, admit them freely, and ask not, "Who's to blame?" or "How can I hide this?" but "What's the lesson here? How can I do

> *Aim for success,*
> *not perfection.*
> *Never give up your right to be wrong,*
> *because then you will lose*
> *the ability to learn new things*
> *and move forward with your life.*
> *Remember that fear*
> *always lurks behind perfectionism.*
> *Confronting your fears and allowing yourself*
> *the right to be human can,*
> *paradoxically,*
> *make you a far happier and*
> *more productive person.*
>
> DR. DAVID M. BURNS

this better?"

The goal becomes excellence, not perfection.

It helps to realize that we're *far* from perfect—we are, in fact, *crazy*. I first realized I was crazy when I was fifteen. I was in the shower brushing my teeth. As was my custom, I spit the toothpaste-gook on the shower floor. By some strange suspension of the law of physics, however, the gook landed on my *foot*.

"Eeeuuuuuu!" I recoiled. The thought of *toothpaste-gook* on my *foot* was *too disgusting* to even *consider*.

And then, from wherever those occasional sane thoughts come, came the thought, "Less than one second before the gook landed on your foot, *it was in your mouth."*

At that moment, I knew I was crazy.

Life has never been the same.

One of the best examples of how strong the taboo against making a mistake has become is the use of the word *sin*. In ancient Roman times, *sin* was a term used in archery. It meant simply *to miss the mark*. At target practice, each shot was either a hit or a sin. If you sinned, you made corrections and tried again.

Today, of course, *sin* means, to quote the *American Heritage,* "A condition of estrangement from God as a result of breaking God's law." Whew. No wonder people try to avoid even "the near occasion" of sin. Some people treat mistakes with the same reverence.

Mistakes are valuable if, for no other reason, they show us what *not* to do. As Joseph Ray told us, "The Athenians, alarmed at the internal decay of their Republic, asked Demosthenes what to do. His reply: 'Do not do what you are doing now.' "

In Hollywood, mis-takes are common. ("That was wonderful, darlings. Now let's get ready for take two.") Give yourself as many re-takes as you need. Stars do it. ("I didn't feel quite right with that one, Mr. deMille. Can we take it again?") Why not you?

A Hollywood song (lyrics by Dorothy Fields) sums it up: "Pick yourself up, dust yourself off, start all over again." Or, to quote an African proverb, "Do not look where you fell, but where you

> *Mistakes are*
> *the portals of discovery.*
>
> JAMES JOYCE

slipped."

If you're learning, growing, and trying new things—expect mistakes. They're a natural part of the learning process. In fact, someone once said, "If you're not making at least fifty mistakes a day, you're not trying hard enough." What the person meant, I think, is that growth, discovery, and expansion have mistakes built into them.

To avoid situations in which you *might* make mistakes may be the biggest mistake of all.

*The best things and best people
rise out of their separateness.
I'm against a homogenized society
because I want the cream to rise.*

ROBERT FROST

*I hate quotations.*

RALPH WALDO EMERSON

# The Two Faces of Anger:
# Guilt and Resentment

Guilt is anger directed at ourselves—at what we did or did not do. Resentment is anger directed at others—at what they did or did not do.

The process of guilt and resentment is the same:

1. We have an image that either we or others should live up to. (An image of all the should's, must's, have-to's, and demands we learned or created about our own and/or others' behavior.)

2. We emotionally demand that we or others live up to this image.

3. We or they fail to live up to our image.

4. We judge the "contrary action" as wrong, bad, evil, wicked, etc.

5. We become emotionally upset—bitter, alienated, hurt, hostile, belligerent, combative, contentious, quarrelsome, vicious, touchy, cranky, cross, grouchy, testy, enraged, aggravated, annoyed, furious, teed-off, etc., etc. We'll put them all under the general umbrella of "angry."

6. We assign blame for the emotional upset—either *we* did it or *they* did it. (The judge pronounces sentence.)

7. The swift execution of justice. If we are to blame, we direct the anger toward ourselves,

> *Every great mistake has*
> *a halfway moment,*
> *a split second when it*
> *can be recalled and*
> *perhaps remedied.*
>
> PEARL S. BUCK

feeling regret, remorse, shame, repentance, culpability, fault—we'll call all that guilt. If the transgressor of our expectations was someone or something other than ourselves, we call our anger spite, jealousy, suspicion, malice, begrudging, covetousness, envy, indignation—all of which we'll call resentment. The sad fact is that, whether we blame *us* or *them, we feel the hurt.* But that is not considered, at least for long.

8. All of this continues for the prescribed length of time and intensity. No reprieves, no appeals—*possible* time off for *very* good behavior.

If these are the two faces of anger, what's the good in that? Frankly, not much. So why do I have anger in a section on Master Teachers? If we had listened to the voices of the Master Teachers *at the very beginning,* the *feelings* of guilt and resentment would not have been necessary. To save us from these is the job of the Master Teacher, anger.

Anger begins as an inner twinge. We sense something long before it blossoms (explodes?) into an emotional tirade. If we listen to this twinge—and follow its advice—the emotional outburst (or inburst) is not needed.

What advice is this Master Teacher giving? Stop, look, and change.

**Stop.** Don't do anything. You are at a choice point. You have two ways to go. One choice equals freedom. The other choice equals misery—familiar misery, but misery nonetheless.

**Look.** What image (expectation, belief, should, must, ought-to) about either yourself or another is about to be (or has recently been) violated? ("People *should* drive carefully." "I *mustn't* eat cake if I'm on a diet.")

**Change.** What do you change? *The image.* Your image *is not accurate*—according to hard, cold, physical evidence. People *should* drive carefully, but do they always? Hardly. That "should" is inaccurate, false, erroneous, wrong. People on diets *mustn't* eat cake, but do they? You bet. That "mustn't" is untrue, faulty, mistaken, and incorrect. Based on the actual life-data given to you, your images (should's, must's, have-to's) are all wet (or don't hold any

> *Everything that irritates us*
> *about others can lead us to*
> *an understanding*
> *of ourselves.*
>
> CARL JUNG

water, or sink in the ocean of truth, or any other aquatic metaphor you choose).

But what do we often do with the image that is proven—conclusively—to be inaccurate? Do we disregard it? Do we intelligently alter it, based on reality? ("People should drive carefully, and sometimes they don't." "People on diets shouldn't eat too much cake too often.") No. We make ourselves miserable with the inaccurate image. The world's actions do not conform to our beliefs. Woe is us. Our own actions don't conform to our beliefs. Woe *on* us.

Can you see the absurdity of this? We demand that our illusion (our image) be more real than reality (what actually happened), hurting ourselves in the process. Where is the victory in that? (I bet you thought that was a rhetorical question. It's not. There are answers.)

First, we get to feel *right*. Feeling right is a strong drug. Some people sacrifice a lot to be right. Ever hear the expression "dead right"? The question the Master Teacher asks with each initial twinge of guilt or resentment: Would you rather be right or be happy? If we answer "Happy," we are free. If we answer "Right," the cycle of misery begins again. If we're right we must punish—either ourselves or another. As I mentioned, the irony is that when we punish another, we first punish ourselves. Who do you think feels all that hate we have for another? The other person? Seldom. Us? Always.

Second, anger is a habit. We learned it early on—before we could walk or talk, in some instances. The habit is so ingrained in some people that they haven't understood a word of this chapter. "What *is* he talking about? When people do something *wrong*, I will *naturally* feel upset. When I do something *bad*, I will *of course* feel guilty." It's not "natural," it's not "of course"; it's learned. If our early lessons of acceptance were as successful as our early lessons of anger, how much happier we would all be.

Third, guilt and resentment give us (and others) permission to do it again. Far from preventing a recurrence, the punishment simply lets the person (either you or another) say, "I've paid my dues; now I'm free to do it again." Many people weigh the

> *The last temptation is*
> *the greatest treason:*
> *To do the right deed*
> *for the wrong reason.*
>
> T. S. ELIOT

guilt they will feel against the pleasure of the forbidden action they want to take. As long as they're willing to "pay the price," the action's okay. People often ponder the anticipated wrath of another before taking certain actions. "If I'm five minutes late, he'll be a little mad." They make a choice between another's resentment and whatever it is that might make them five minutes late. If they're willing to endure the chastisement, they reason, it's okay to be late. Guilt and resentment, then, far from preventing "evil,"* perpetuate it.

*"EVIL" is "LIVE" spelled backwards.

What if we use the twinge of guilt to change the *action*? What if we feel the guilt and *don't* eat the cake? Isn't this using the Master Teacher's message for our good?

Well, it's a good start. If we don't do something because we're afraid of the guilt, we are, in fact, being motivated by fear and guilt. If we do good because we fear what might happen to us if we don't do good, the act of good is tainted with fear. As a transition—especially when breaking a habit—it's a beginning, but we must move beyond that or we find ourselves in the trap of not feeling guilty because we'd feel guilty if we felt guilty.

So what can we use to motivate ourselves to do good? Do good because good is the right thing to do. Not right as "conforming to law and morality (or else)," but right as "in accordance with fact, reason, and truth."

Another great motivator is love. Love yourself enough to stay on the diet because you love your body and want to keep it healthy.

More on this and other positive motivators later, along with the cure for guilt and resentment.

The cure for guilt and resentment? Forgiveness. The preventative? Acceptance. The best reason to do good? Loving.

And if you forget any of this, the Master Teacher will be there, just before you veer off-course, asking gently, with that first twinge of guilt or resentment, "Would you rather be right or be happy?"

*It is easier
to get forgiveness
than permission.*

STUART'S LAW OF RETROACTION

Your answer will always be respected.

*The most important thing
is to be <u>whatever</u> you are
without shame.*

ROD STEIGER

*Don't be afraid to take
a big step
if one is indicated.
You can't cross a chasm in
two small jumps.*

DAVID LLOYD GEORGE

# Fear

When entering a new situation, wouldn't it be wonderful to have an extra burst of energy? Wouldn't it be nice if our senses sharpened, our mind became more alert, and we felt a sense of increased readiness? Wouldn't it be great if we breathed a little deeper, getting more oxygen; our heart beat a little faster, getting that oxygen around our body; and our eyes widened a little, allowing us to see more clearly?

Wouldn't that be a nice gift to have? That would be a Master Teacher worth welcoming, right?

Well, we have that gift already. It's called fear.

Fear? Sure. If you think about it (or perhaps I should say *feel* about it), the only difference between "fear" and "excitement" is what we label it. The two are pretty much the same physiological/emotional reaction. With fear, we put a negative spin on it: "Oh, no!" With excitement, we give it some positive english: "Oh, boy!"

Why does fear have such a bad rep? Childhood. Our parents used fear to keep us safe when we were out of their sight. As children, we didn't know the difference between playing in the street and playing on a playground; we didn't know the difference between poison and milk; we didn't know the difference between a total stranger and a perfect stranger. Our parents taught us—with the most loving intentions—to fear *everything* new. This fear probably saved our lives on any number of

> *Everyone has talent.*
> *What is rare is the courage*
> *to follow the talent to the*
> *dark place where it leads.*
>
> ERICA JONG

occasions.

All well and good. The problem is, at the age of, say, eighteen, when we *did* know the difference between the truly dangerous and the merely intriguing, no one taught us to use fear for the remarkable gift it is. It's as though nobody took the training wheels off our bike.

Today, we probably don't need to fear poison to keep us from drinking it. We don't drink it because, well, there's no future in it. Only occasionally do we need the rush of fear necessary to quickly avoid a new situation (an imperfect stranger on a dark street, for example). Most of the time, however, fear is a wonderful ally in our quest for growth, learning, and expansion.

To use fear as the friend it is, we must retrain and reprogram ourselves. (Enough blaming the past. Your life is in *your* hands now.) We must persistently and convincingly tell ourselves that the fear is here—with its gift of energy and heightened awareness—so we can do our best and learn the most in the new situation.

Before we can make friends with fear, it may be necessary to learn that fear is not the enemy. It's important to know that, if we do the thing we fear, we will not die. Some people tell themselves, of every new situation, "It's going to be awful and terrible and then I'll die." The phrase "to die of embarrassment" is an example of the exaggerations people make about fear.

To prove to ourselves we won't die—that, in fact, nothing physically bad is likely to happen to us—it's necessary to move *through* the fear. Most people treat fear as a wall at the edge of their comfort zone. As they approach the wall, the fear increases, and they turn around and walk away. They do not do whatever they fear. Hence, the belief that fear is a limitation, and not a prelude to illumination, is perpetuated.

If you want to learn about fear, whatever it is you fear doing, that is the very next thing to do. Fear is not a wall; it's just an emotion. Move *through* the fear. Keep taking step after step toward the thing you want. It may become quite uncomfortable; then, suddenly, it will be less.

Once you start doing the thing you fear, the fear

> *When you feel in your gut*
> *what you are and then*
> *dynamically pursue it—*
> *don't back down and don't give up—*
> *then you're going*
> *to mystify a lot of folks.*
>
> BOB DYLAN

is used for its true purpose: extra energy. We use the energy doing what we want to do, and the "wall" of fear disappears.

Over time, you'll learn to use the energy even before you start moving—you'll create a gate for yourself in the wall. Then, when the fear arises, you'll say, "Welcome. I needed a little extra energy. This one might be a challenge!" And off into the sunrise you'll go with your old friend.

*To accomplish our destiny
it is not enough to merely
guard prudently
against road accidents.
We must also cover before nightfall
the distance assigned
to each of us.*

ALEXIS CARREL

*If I had a formula*
*for bypassing trouble,*
*I would not pass it round.*
*Trouble creates*
*a capacity to handle it.*
*I don't embrace trouble;*
*that's as bad as treating it*
*as an enemy.*
*But I do say meet it as a friend,*
*for you'll see a lot of it*
*and had better be*
*on speaking terms with it.*

OLIVER WENDELL HOLMES

# Pain and Dis-ease

Imagine this scenario: You have a very important appointment at 9:00 a.m. The night before, you tell your two roommates, who are also two of your best friends, "I have an important meeting tomorrow morning. It means a lot to me. Would you please make sure I'm awake by 8:00 a.m.?" Your friends, knowing your history of sleeping late, are reluctant. "Please do it," you implore, "It's very important. Do whatever you have to, just make sure I'm up by 8:00 a.m." Your friends agree.

The next morning at 7:00, they knock on your door. You do not respond. Five minutes later they knock harder. No response. Five minutes later they knock and yell. No response. Ten minutes later they come into your room and yell. No response. Five minutes later they gently shake you. You tell them to leave you alone. You've changed your mind. The appointment's not so important after all. Knowing you well, they do not believe you. They shake you and call your name. You tell them you are awake. They are not convinced. They check back in ten minutes: still asleep. As 8:00 a.m. approaches, they shake you, yelling, "Wake up!" You are not pleased. Your friends are threatening cold water. Eventually, reluctantly—if your friends are good enough (i.e., persistent enough)—you wake up.

What if this were the role pain and dis-ease played in your life? We may not remember giving a wake-up call, and we may not remember asking them to do the awakening, but doing it they are.

> *Whenever he*
> *thought about it,*
> *he felt terrible.*
> *And so, at last, he came to*
> *a fateful decision.*
> *He decided*
> *not to think about it.*

What are we waking up to? Ourselves. Living in the moment. Living more effectively. Better relationships with ourselves and others. And so on. When we're "asleep," we are unconscious and not aware of these possibilities. Our friends know we want to be aware of them, and so our friends go through the thankless job of waking us up.

Pain (any pain—emotional, physical, mental) has a message. The information it has about our life can be remarkably specific, but it usually falls into one of two categories: "We would be more alive if we did more of this," and, "Life would be more lovely if we did less of that." Once we get the pain's message, and follow its advice, the pain goes away.

You can use your sanctuary to find out what your pain is trying to tell you. You can, for example, contact the pain through the information retrieval system. Or you could have it appear on the video screen. You might have to "consult" with it in the health center. You can invite it in on the people mover.

Imagine the pain as though it were animated by Walt Disney, or as a Muppet. Give it a mouth. Let it speak. Remember, this is a friend. Ask it a few questions. For example:

What do I get from having you around? What excuses do you give me? What information do you have for me? What should I be doing less often? What should I be doing more often? How can I take better care of my body? How can I take better care of my emotions? What can I do to take better care of my mind? What can I do to take better care of myself?

After you've had your chat, thank the pain for the information, surround it with white light, and see it dissolve into that light. Then fill the place in your body/mind/emotions where the pain was with white light.

It is important to follow the pain's advice. Remember, painful = PAY-IN-FULL. The more severe the pain or illness, the more severe will be the necessary changes. These may involve breaking bad habits, or acquiring some new and better ones. To hear the advice of the pain without following it is as useful (or should I say useless?) as any other unheeded good advice. Take the corrective action nec-

> *We contain an internal world*
> *which is just as active*
> *and complicated*
> *as the one we live in.*
>
> JONATHAN MILLER, M.D.

essary, and the pain will decrease. Continue this healing-through-action, and you will be healed.

How far will pain go to get its message across? Illness. Dis-ease. The ultimate wake-up call is a life-threatening illness. If that alarm clock in your ear doesn't wake you up, nothing will.*

---

*My book on this subject, *You Can't Afford the Luxury of a Negative Thought: A Book for People with Any Life-Threatening Illness—Including Life,* is available by calling 1-800-LIFE-101.

*The body never lies.*

MARTHA GRAHAM

*It's a funny thing about life;
if you refuse to accept
anything but the best,
you very often get it.*

SOMERSET MAUGHAM

# Stubbornness

Gather 'round rebels, this chapter's especially for you. (Considering my temperament, I should probably say "me.")

Many of us rebels got into the rebellion business for good reason—we were rebels with a cause. As children, when the world moved in with its obsession for conformity ("We'd love you a lot more if only you were a little less different"), the rebels said, "I won't," and stuck to it.

The defense of our individuality continued—probably necessarily so—through formal schooling (Ugh!). Eventually, it became a habit. We became masters of "won't power." Give us something to be *against* and we shine. As soon as what we're against has gone, we're lost.

Rebels without something to be against are a sad sight. They wander around. They mutter to themselves. They secretly hope something will go wrong so they can be against it. Like professional soldiers in peacetime, rebels would probably be very unhappy in Utopia.

Fortunately, there *is* a solution. Just as fear is also excitement, stubbornness is also *determination*. It's simply a matter of shifting from "won't power" to "will power."

Rather than "I won't get sick," change it to "I *will* keep my mind, body, and emotions healthy." Replace "I won't be with people who don't understand me," with "I *will* be with people who like me

> *Anyone can revolt.*
> *It is more difficult silently to obey*
> *our own inner promptings,*
> *and to spend our lives finding sincere*
> *and fitting means of expression*
> *for our temperament*
> *and our gifts.*
>
> GEORGES ROUAULT

as I am." Turn "I hate war," to "I love peace."

It's a matter of finding the positive opposite (and rebels are *so* good at finding opposites) and focusing on that. This shifts the energy from stubbornness to determination.

My only problem: how do I communicate all this to my fellow rebels in a way they won't rebel against?

*Let us, then, be up and doing,*
*With a heart for any fate;*
*Still achieving, still pursuing,*
*Learn to labor and to wait.*

HENRY WADSWORTH LONGFELLOW

1839

*When you stop drinking,*
*you have to deal with this*
*marvelous personality*
*that started you drinking*
*in the first place.*

JIMMY BRESLIN

# Subtracting Addiction

We've all got one—an addiction, that is. There are the well-known addictions: drugs, alcohol, smoking, gambling. There are the less-known-but-getting-more-well-known-each-day addictions: food, sex, romance, work, religion, spirituality—almost anything good can be turned bad by obsession and lack of moderation. Some people are addicted to their negative thoughts and the feelings those thoughts produce.

Some minimize their addictions by calling them "bad habits." Others deny addiction and seemingly become addicted to denial. Many, who wouldn't dream of having an addiction, are addicted to normalcy. We all have one.

An addiction is anything that has more power over you than you do. If it "runs" you, it's an addiction. If you're not sure it's addiction, stop doing it. If you can stop for an indefinite period of time, then it's a preference, not an addiction. If you can't—or can't even conceive of giving it (them) up—that's addiction.

The "old" word for addiction was *temptation*. "Lead us not into temptation" (Jesus); "My temptation is quiet" (Yeats); "I can resist everything except temptation" (Oscar Wilde).

One of the most successful programs for overcoming addiction is the Twelve Steps. Originally created to help alcoholics, the Twelve Steps have been adapted to every known addiction. The pro-

> *Why comes temptation,*
> *but for man to meet*
> *And master and make crouch*
> *beneath his foot,*
> *And so be pedestaled in triumph?*
>
> ROBERT BROWNING

gram has benefited millions.

## THE TWELVE STEPS

1. We admitted we were powerless over our addiction—that our lives had become unmanageable.

2. Came to believe that a Power greater than ourselves could restore us to sanity.

3. Made a decision to turn our will and our lives over to the care of this Higher Power, *as we understood Him, Her, or It.*

4. Made a searching and fearless moral inventory of ourselves.

5. Admitted to our Higher Power, to ourselves, and to another human being the exact nature of our wrongs.

6. Were entirely ready to have our Higher Power remove all these defects of character.

7. Humbly asked our Higher Power to remove our shortcomings.

8. Made a list of all persons we had harmed, and became willing to make amends to them all.

9. Made direct amends to such people wherever possible, except when to do so would injure them or others.

10. Continued to take personal inventory and when we were wrong, promptly admitted it.

11. Sought, through prayer and meditation, to improve our conscious contact with our Higher Power *as we understood Him, Her, or It,* praying only for knowledge of our Higher Power's will for us and the power to carry that out.

12. Having had a spiritual awakening as the result of these steps, we tried to carry this message to others and to practice these principles in all our affairs.

Once you overcome your addiction, you know you can overcome all things. The impossible becomes possible. The undoable, doable. The unmanageable, manageable. Overcoming an addiction even eases the process of releasing our addiction to life at the time of our death.

In the process of overcoming addiction, you can learn discipline, self-confidence, humility, apprecia-

> *Blessed is the man*
> *that endureth temptation:*
> *for when he is tried,*
> *he shall receive the crown of life.*

JAMES

1:12

tion, self-love, and forgiveness. Important lessons, these. That's why I consider addiction one of the Master Teachers in disguise.

*A good many young writers*
*make the mistake of enclosing*
*a stamped, self-addressed envelope,*
*big enough for the manuscript*
*to come back in.*
*This is too much of a*
*temptation to the editor.*

RING LARDNER

*Perhaps the most valuable result*
*of all education*
*is the ability to make yourself*
*do the thing you have to do*
*when it ought to be done,*
*whether you like it or not;*
*it is the first lesson*
*that ought to be learned;*
*and however early*
*a man's training begins,*
*it is probably the last lesson*
*that he learns thoroughly.*

THOMAS HUXLEY

# Depression

The word *depression* is used to describe two distinct maladies. One use is to express *disappointment:* "They didn't return my phone calls. I'm depressed."* "How depressing—the coffee machine is out of *cafe olé.*" We also feel this mild kind of depression in the normal cycle of life's ups and downs.

The other use of the word *depression* is medical—it describes a physical illness caused by a biological (yes, usually genetic) imbalance in the body.

The simple solution for disappointment depression: Get up and get moving. *Physically* move. Do. Act. Get going.

Depression is often caused by a sense of not having accomplished enough. We question the usefulness of what we've achieved in the past, and doubt our ability to achieve anything useful in the future. Self-doubt robs us of our energy. We feel depressed.

We look at all we want to do. It seems overwhelming. We tell ourselves, "I can't do all this," and instantly fulfill our own prophecy by not even trying. The energy drops even more, and the depression deepens.

When we eventually feel we *must* do something,

*A severe loss can trigger a form of depression that is a natural part of the healing process. (Please see the chapter "Good Mourning.")

> *I was once thrown out*
> *of a mental hospital*
> *for depressing the other patients.*

OSCAR LEVANT

there seems to be so much left undone from our previous inertia that we become confused. The confusion leads to indecision. The indecision leads to, "Oh, what's the use," and more inaction, which leads to...you guessed it.

At some point, the cycle must be broken by action. Do something—*anything*—physical. If the house is a mess, pick up *one thing*—*any* one thing—and *do* something with it: put it away, throw it out, send it to your brother, donate it to charity, something, *anything*. Pick up one more thing. Continue. Eventually, you will have a clean house. Before "eventually," however, the depression will begin to lift.

Yes, disappointment depression is a Master Teacher. Its message is, "Get moving. The energy is here. Use it." When you start to move, the energy will meet your movement. But first, you must move.

Medical ("clinical") depression is not caused by disappointment or lack of action, but by a biological imbalance in the chemistry of the brain. This form of depression takes a bit more explaining— there are *so many* misconceptions about it. Here's my story.

Over an almost-thirty-year period, I had attended more personal growth workshops, visited more healers, meditated more hours, taken more vitamins, and not only read but written more self-help books than almost anyone I knew. Nevertheless, I was not happy. I wasn't even satisfied. I wasn't even simply bored.

I was miserable.

By mid-1993, I was ready to try anything—even psychiatry. I called Harold H. Bloomfield, M.D., one of my co-authors on *How to Survive the Loss of a Love,* told him I wanted to make a professional appointment, and met him at his office. We spoke for an hour. Finally, he said, "Peter, you've been suffering!"

Yeah. That's what I was doing—although I had never applied the word *suffering* to myself. His official diagnosis: depression.

Like many people, I had some serious misconceptions about depression. I didn't *like* depression. I

> *The tricks that work on others*
> *count for nothing in that*
> *very well-lit back alley where one*
> *keeps assignations with oneself:*
> *No winning smiles will do here,*
> *no prettily drawn lists*
> *of good intentions.*
>
> JOAN DIDION

didn't *want* depression. But then, I guess you don't get to pick your disease.

To my surprise, I learned that depression was a physical illness, a biochemical imbalance in the brain most likely caused by certain neurotransmitters (the fluid the brain uses to communicate with itself) being pumped away too soon. When there are too few of certain neurotransmitters, brain function becomes inharmonious, and the complex mental, emotional, and physical manifestations of depression result.

These manifestations can include a "down" feeling, fatigue, sleep disorders, physical aches and pains, eating irregularities, listening to Julio Iglesias, irritability, difficulty concentrating, feeling worthless, guilt, addictions (attempts to self-medicate the pain away), suicidal thoughts, and my favorite, anhedonia.

*Anhedonia* means "the inability to experience pleasure." The original title for Woody Allen's movie *Annie Hall* was *Anne Hedonia*—the perfect description of Woody Allen's character. It was also the description of my life. Although I had spikes of happiness, nothing gave me pleasure for any length of time. The concept of "just being" was entirely foreign to me. My intensive self-help seeking since 1965 had been my attempt to obtain the simple enjoyment of living that many people seemed to have naturally.

All my attempts had been unsuccessful—I had a *physical illness* that prevented even the best-built self-esteem structure from standing very long. In the book Harold and I later wrote, *How to Heal Depression,* the chapter explaining this phenomenon is entitled, "The Power of Positive Thinking Crashes and Burns in the Face of Depression." You can plant all the personal growth seeds you want, but they become like the seeds that fell on the rock in Jesus' parable (Matthew 13:5–6):

> Some [seed] fell on rocky places, where it did not have much soil. It sprang up quickly, because the soil was shallow. But when the sun came up, the plants were scorched, and they withered because they had no root.

That's what depression had wrought inside me: one, vast, barren rock garden—without the garden.

> *There is surely a piece of*
> *divinity in us,*
> *something that was*
> *before the elements,*
> *and owes no homage*
> *unto the sun.*
>
> SIR THOMAS BROWNE
>
> 1642

I also learned that most depression is inherited. I realized that if I looked around my family tree and saw a lot of nuts, there was a very good chance I was not a passion fruit (which is *just* what I thought I was). Since depression is a genetic biological illness, like diabetes or low thyroid, it wasn't lack of character, laziness, or something I could "snap out of"—it would be like trying to snap out of a toothache. This meant the dozens of other causes for depression given to me by John-Roger and other quacks in his cult were invalid, too.*

I was ready to consider what the good Doctor Bloomfield recommended I do about my depression.

He explained several options, which included two short-term "talk" therapies (Cognitive Therapy and Interpersonal Therapy) and antidepressants—as in Prozac. I, who had been programmed by John-Roger to think drugs were the devil's own tool, thought—as many people did—that Prozac was the devil itself.

The Church of Scientology had done a brilliant job programming the media and, hence, the general public, into believing that not only was Prozac unsafe, but *astonishingly* unsafe. They accomplished this (for whatever reason) by finding a handful of people who had done some aberrant things. Scientology then presented the aberrant behavior of these people as typical side effects of Prozac. It was a thoroughly imbalanced and unscientific presentation. More than five million people take Prozac in this country every day—ten million worldwide. Millions more have used Prozac since its introduction in 1987. It is among the safest of all prescribed medications. (No one has ever died from taking Prozac—although hundreds die each year from allergic reactions to penicillin, or from internal bleeding caused by aspirin.)

Still, I didn't like the idea of taking a pill that would—as *Newsweek* pointed out on its cover—give

---

**For the story of my fifteen years of cult life—and its aftermath—please read *LIFE 102: What to Do When Your Guru Sues You*. Available at your local bookstore or by calling 1-800-LIFE-101.

> *A depressed person is someone who,*
> *if he is in the bath,*
> *will not get out*
> *to answer the telephone.*
>
> QUENTIN CRISP

me a different personality. I didn't necessarily like the personality I had, but I also didn't want to become a *Stepford* writer.

Harold explained that antidepressant medications do not give one a new personality. There is no "high" connected to them. They're not tranquilizers, pep pills, or mood elevators. All antidepressants do is keep the brain from pumping away certain neurotransmitters too quickly. This allows the neurotransmitters to rise to appropriate levels, which lets the brain function harmoniously again.

An analogy might be that antidepressants plug a hole in a rain barrel so the barrel can fill. The depression lifts because the brain's naturally produced neurotransmitters are allowed to rise to natural levels. Antidepressant medications, then, don't add a synthetic chemical to the brain that alters the brain's function; they merely keep the brain from pumping away its own naturally produced neurotransmitters too quickly.

Further, if you take antidepressants and feel better, it's *because you are depressed.* If you take an antidepressant and are not depressed, you won't feel much of anything. In this, antidepressants are like aspirin: if you have a headache and take an aspirin, your headache goes away and you feel better. If you don't have a headache and take an aspirin, you won't feel much different. The good feelings touted so enthusiastically by people taking antidepressants are not *caused* by the antidepressant medication, but by the lifting of the depression—when a pain you've grown accustomed to goes away, the feeling of just plain "ordinary" can seem like euphoria.

Okay. I was ready. Lay on the Prozac.

Within a week of beginning the medication, I felt not exactly better, but as though the bottom of my emotional pit had been raised. In the past, small setbacks had caused a toboggan ride all the way down to an emotional state best described as "What's the point of living?" In the choice between life and death, I would reluctantly choose life (with about the same enthusiasm as Michelangelo's Adam on the Sistine Chapel receiving the spark of life from God), and crawl back up to "normal" again.

Normal for me, however, *was* depression. As it

> *If Quentin Crisp had never existed*
> *it is unlikely that anyone*
> *would have had the nerve*
> *to invent him.*
>
> ANONYMOUS REVIEWER

turns out, I've had a long-term, low-grade depression since I was three. This depressed state was my benchmark for "normal." On top of this, I would have, from time to time, major depressive episodes—lasting from six months to more than a year. When the two of these played together (that is, played havoc together on me), I had what is known in psychiatric circles as a *double depression* (a fate I would not wish upon my worst enemy).

After I'd taken Prozac for two weeks, I felt the floor of my dungeon had risen even higher. By the third week, I felt I had—for the first time—some level ground on which to build my life. I still was concerned how firm it was, so I walked across it lightly, as one does across a piece of land that was once quicksand.

That was the image I had: any good deed, any positive project, any accomplishment, I placed on the quicksand where—like Janet Leigh's car in *Psycho*—it would slowly, painfully, inexorably sink.

Now I inched a little farther toward the center of my land, seeing how *firma* the *terra* really was. It was a great victory when I could jump up and down in what was once my pool of emotional quicksand and know it was finally safe to build there.

What I built, of course, was up to me: if I built depressing things, my life would still be depressing. But now I had a chance to build something stable, something reliable, something good.

I also began feeling *spiritual* for the first time. I felt connected to God in a solid, unpretentious way. The discovery of this connection was no great "hooray, hooray, I found God," but a slow clarification—like watching a Polaroid picture develop. It all seemed so natural—and simple. It had nothing to do with John-Roger's intricate cosmology I had so carefully memorized.

And—just as so many other great teachers had said—the kingdom of God was within.

I also found myself simply *enjoying* things: ordinary, everyday, no-big-deal activities were *pleasurable*. I remember sitting in a chair, waiting for a table at a restaurant, and I was enjoying just sitting there. I felt so contented, all alone, sitting there, it

> *To love oneself*
> *is the beginning of*
> *a lifelong romance.*
>
> OSCAR WILDE

was almost like being in love.

In fact, it seemed that I *was* falling in love—with myself.

Are *you* depressed? Well, here's a checklist from the National Institutes of Health. On this checklist they also give symptoms of *mania,* which is the irrational, unpredictable upperswing of manic depression. (I never had mania, but I *did* overachieve as a compensation for the depression—I was trying to "prove" my worthiness by outward achievement. Doesn't work.)

According to the National Institutes of Health:

> A thorough diagnosis is needed if four or
> more of the symptoms of depression or ma-

nia persist for more than two weeks or are interfering with work or family life.

With available treatment, eighty percent of the people with serious depression—even those with the most severe forms—can improve significantly. Symptoms can be relieved, usually in a matter of weeks.

**Symptoms of Depression Can Include**

☐ Persistent sad or "empty" mood
☐ Loss of interest or pleasure in ordinary activities, including sex
☐ Decreased energy, fatigue, being "slowed down"
☐ Sleep disturbances (insomnia, early-morning waking, or oversleeping)
☐ Eating disturbances (loss of appetite and weight, or weight gain)
☐ Difficulty concentrating, remembering, making decisions
☐ Feelings of guilt, worthlessness, helplessness
☐ Thoughts of death or suicide, suicide attempts
☐ Irritability
☐ Excessive crying
☐ Chronic aches and pains that don't respond to treatment

**In the Workplace, Symptoms of Depression Often May Be Recognized by**

☐ Decreased productivity
☐ Morale problems
☐ Lack of cooperation
☐ Safety problems, accidents
☐ Absenteeism

> *Never go to a doctor*
> *whose office plants*
> *have died.*
>
> ERMA BOMBECK

- [ ] Frequent complaints of being tired all the time
- [ ] Complaints of unexplained aches and pains
- [ ] Alcohol and drug abuse

**Symptoms of Mania Can Include**

- [ ] Excessively "high" mood
- [ ] Irritability
- [ ] Decreased need for sleep
- [ ] Increased energy and activity
- [ ] Increased talking, moving, and sexual activity
- [ ] Racing thoughts
- [ ] Disturbed ability to make decisions
- [ ] Grandiose notions
- [ ] Being easily distracted

These symptoms are not "just life." If you've had four or more of them for more than two weeks, or *any* of them is interfering with your work or relationships (including with yourself), a diagnosis is in order.

Even if you checked every box (as I must have—I could have been depression's poster boy), you are not *necessarily* depressed. This is simply a checklist to see if a diagnosis from a physician (an M.D., D.O., or psychiatrist) is in order. Your physician may say you're not depressed, but you do (for example) have low thyroid (which mimics depression symptoms in about twenty percent of the cases). This is why a *physician* should be consulted for diagnosis.

On the other hand, emotional support and the administration of short-term "talk" therapies—such as Cognitive or Interpersonal Therapy—is often best given by psychologists (Ph.D.s or MFCCs).

*Death is a friend of ours;*
*and he that is not ready*
*to entertain him*
*is not at home.*

FRANCIS BACON

# Death

Death is an enormous taboo. It's difficult to discuss death without people giggling nervously, becoming entirely too somber, or saying something like, *"Death?* You're going to talk about *death?* Such bad taste!"

When I tell people that in this chapter we will explore the idea that death is a *friend*—a joyful, freeing process—they're liable to think I'm mad. Well, I've been thought mad before—by experts. I figure in 1,000 years, we'll all be dead. What difference does it make what people say about us today? So why not enjoy ourselves while we're alive?

That's precisely the point of death.

In our culture, death is unmentionable. No one ever *dies*. People pass away, pass over, are gone, asleep, at peace, at rest, expired, or departed *(dearly)*.

Many people feel "icky" thinking about death— so they don't. Who, after all, wants to feel icky? They begin to associate icky with death. Then they *know* that death is icky. One should, therefore, not think about death, because there's lots of time to feel icky after you're dead.

This is about as much logic as most people apportion to death. The problem is, if we don't consider death, we are not fully prepared to consider life. Which brings us to our Pop Quiz on death:

**Who said this? "We need to be reminded that there is nothing morbid**

*Thus, thus, it is joy to pass*
*to the world below.*

VIRGIL
70–19 B.C.

*One of the situations in which*
*everybody seems to fear loneliness is death.*
*In tones drenched with pity,*
*people say of someone,*
*"He died alone."*
*I have never understood this point of view.*
*Who wants to have to die*
*and be polite at the same time?*

QUENTIN CRISP

about honestly confronting the fact of life's end, and preparing for it so that we may go gracefully and peacefully. The fact is, we cannot truly face life until we have learned to face the fact that it will be taken away from us."

(A) Mohandas K. Gandhi

(B) Woody Allen

(C) Thomas Mann

(D) Mark Twain

(E) Billy Graham

(F) Charlie Chaplin

(G) Vladimir Nabokov

(H) Emily Dickinson

(I) John Keats

Answer to Pop Quiz (with commentary):

Gandhi said about death, "We do not know whether it is good to live or to die. Therefore, we should not take delight in living nor should we tremble at the thought of death. We should be equiminded towards both. This is the ideal."

Woody Allen wrote, "Death is one of the few things that can be done as easily lying down. The difference between sex and death is that with death you can do it alone and no one is going to make fun of you."

Thomas Mann pointed out, "The only religious way to think of death is as part and parcel of life; to regard it, with the understanding and the emotions, as the inviolable condition of life."

Mark Twain, near death in 1910, wrote, "Death, the only immortal who treats us all alike, whose pity and whose peace and whose refuge are for all—the soiled and the pure, the rich and the poor, the loved and the unloved."

Charlie Chaplin (you thought I was kidding? Would I kid about death? Sure. But would I kid about Chaplin? Never.) said, "Beauty is an omnipresence of death and loveliness, a smiling sadness that we discern in nature and all things, a mystic communion that the poet feels."

Vladimir Nabokov told us, "Life is a great surprise. I do not see why death should not be an even greater one."

Emily Dickinson, a full twenty-three years before her death, rhymed,

*Men fear death as children fear to go in the dark;*
*and as that natural fear in children is increased*
*with tales, so is the other.*

FRANCIS BACON
1625

*Death is just*
*nature's way of telling you,*
*"Hey, you're not alive anymore."*

BULL
NIGHT COURT

Because I could not stop for Death,
He kindly stopped for me—
The Carriage held but just Ourselves
And Immortality.

John Keats mixed death and courtship when wooing Fanny Brawne. On July 25, 1819, he wrote her, "I have two luxuries to brood over in my walks, your loveliness and the hour of my death. O that I could have possession of them both in the same minute." (What woman could resist?)

The answer, then, to our Pop Quiz is (E) Billy Graham.

Why, then, if all these great people had nifty things to say about death, do we as a culture fear it so?

Once again, we return to those thrilling days of childhood. Most people experienced another's death in childhood. Someone (or a pet) they knew as an active, warm, animated being was suddenly an unmoving, cold, silent corpse. This death stuff did not look like much fun.

"Why is he lying in that box? Why are they going to put him in the ground (or burn him)? If he's gone to God, why are you so sad?" In the grief, commotion, and exhaustion that surrounds dying and its aftermath, a child's questions about death are seldom properly answered.

The more people a child asks, the more conflicting the answers may become. Children are little curiosity machines. They know how to ask all the "right" questions—the ones most adults haven't yet figured out for themselves. In the dialogue between children and adults, only sex is shrouded in as much mystery, embarrassment, and confusion as death.

If the person (or pet) who died was close to the child, then he or she will associate death with the intense pain of life's first significant loss. Death, then, is associated with hurt. The child also sees how the adults behave at death: weeping, wailing, suffering. This death thing must be pretty terrible.

If, in childhood, the death of another took place after a long illness, all the disagreeableness of the dying process—hospitals, infirmities, unpleasant sights and smells—is associated with death itself. To a child, seeing someone gradually get sicker and in more pain seems to mean that, after death, the sick-

> *Sleep after toil,*
> *port after stormy seas,*
> *Ease after war,*
> *death after life*
> *does greatly please.*

EDMUND SPENSER

1590

ness and pain will worsen.

This description doesn't even include the hell-is-waiting-for-you, burning-sulphur, fire-and-brimstone religious training some children get. A child, hearing a list of sins, soon realizes, "If this is all I have to do to go to hell, *I'm going to hell.*"

It's little wonder that children put the subject of death on hold. Like homework, if they don't have to think about it, they won't. Many people stopped thinking about death in childhood and haven't sincerely considered it since.

This means that many adults hold a child's view of death. Let's see if we can reeducate that part of ourselves—to mature about death.

Of course, one's belief about what happens *after* death falls into The Gap. There are, however, only three major beliefs about death in the entire Gap. One of these views fits almost every religious, spiritual, philosophical, agnostic, and atheistic group in The Gap.

Interestingly, none of these beliefs has much bad stuff to say about death to the average adult follower of that belief. If there is any nastiness after death, it's going to happen to *them* (the nonbelievers), not to *us* (the believers). To a child, certain aspects of some beliefs might appear terrifying, but to an adult, there's nothing to fear. (In fact, in many cases, death is rather appealing.)

Although I stay away from Gap matters as a rule, I will make this one suggestion for you to follow while exploring your Gap: Live by what you believe so fully that your life blossoms, or else purge the fear-and-guilt-producing beliefs from your life.

When people believe one thing and do another, they are inviting misery. If you give yourself the name, play the game. When you believe something you don't follow with your heart, intellect, and body, it hurts. Don't do that. Live your belief, or let that belief go.

If you're not actively living a belief, it's not really *your* belief, anyway—you're just kidding yourself. If you're not actively involved in getting what you want, you don't really want it. You probably *really* believe something else, but may be afraid to admit it to yourself.

> *As a well-spent day*
> *brings happy sleep,*
> *so life well used*
> *brings happy death.*
>
> LEONARDO DA VINCI

> *Immortality*
> *consists largely*
> *of boredom.*
>
> COCHRANE
> *STAR TREK*

Let's take a look at each of the three beliefs about death from an adult point of view. If, as a child, you were told you'd know more about death "when you're older," I offer this one thought: you're older now.

**Life is purely biological.** Once the brain stops working, our sense of aliveness is no more, and that's it. As Dr. Albert Ellis, a proponent of this school of thought, pointed out with his characteristic candor and clarity, "When you're dead, you're f—ing dead!"

The idea of "being no more" may frighten a child. Children associate nothingness with the dark. The dark usually frightens a child. Therefore death is frightening.

Many adults can probably agree with William Hazlitt:

> Perhaps the best cure for the fear of death is to reflect that life has a beginning as well as an end. There was a time when we were not: this gives us no concern—why then should it trouble us that a time will come when we shall cease to be? I have no wish to be alive a hundred years ago, why should I regret and lay it so much to heart that I shall not be here a hundred years hence?

If this is a purely biological life, then who would want to live forever anyway? Imagine living forever, and ever, and ever, and ever, and ever, and ever, and ever, and ever, and ever. If you got bored reading all those "ever's," imagine how quickly you would become bored with an eternal life in a finite universe.

Think about it: if you had infinite time but finite space, eventually you would have explored and experienced every "thing" there was to explore and experience. And then you'd get to start over, and over, and over, and over, and over, and over, and over, and over.

If you've ever gotten bored with anything you once found fascinating, you understand the problem. Given enough time, you would become bored with everything in life.

Infinity is enough time.

After enough time, you would find yourself agreeing with the person who, in 1990 B.C., wrote,

> *For God so loved the world,*
> *that he gave*
> *his only begotten Son,*
> *that whosoever believeth in him*
> *should not perish,*
> *but have everlasting life.*
>
> *For God sent not*
> *his son into the world*
> *to condemn the world;*
> *but that the world through him*
> *might be saved.*
>
> JOHN
> 3:16–17

Death is in my sight today
As when a man desires to see home
When he has spent many years in captivity.

It's from a poem called *The Man Who Was Tired of Life*.

Or, as Mark Twain explained, "Whoever has lived long enough to find out what life is, knows how deep a debt of gratitude we owe to Adam, the first great benefactor of our race. He brought death into the world."

I end the exploration of this portion of The Gap with the words of Albert Einstein: "The fear of death is the most unjustified of all fears, for there is no risk of accident to someone who's dead."

**When you die, you go to heaven or hell.** This life is a one-shot opportunity. If we're good, we get paradise forever. If we're bad, we go to hell forever. (Catholics include a pre-heaven condition, purgatory, for those who weren't bad enough for hell, but are not yet good enough for heaven.)

This sounds pretty good. Eternal paradise. Now, this wouldn't become tiresome because, as far as I know, heaven is infinite, and, as far as I know, we are not saddled with physical bodies. This wouldn't be boring. This would be eternal bliss.

"Life is eternal," Rossiter Raymond wrote in his *Commendatory Prayer*, "and love is immortal; and death is only a horizon; and a horizon is nothing save the limit of our sight."

In this belief of death, you rest after a careworn life, but you rest not in nothingness, but in paradise. God, James Johnson imagines, uses death as a sort of chauffeur for the Divine Rest Limo Company. God orders death:

Find Sister Caroline
And she's tired—
She's weary—
Go down, Death, and bring her to me.

Thomas Fuller, in his 1642 *Life of Monica*, tells of the saint's death: "Drawing near her death, she sent most pious thoughts as harbingers to heaven; and her soul saw a glimpse of happiness through the chinks of her sickness-broken body."

The Bible, in both the Old and New Testaments, has many nice things to say about death. Ecclesi-

> *Death is a low chemical*
> *trick played on everybody*
> *except sequoia trees.*
>
> J. J. FURNAS

astes 7:1 tells us, "The day of death [is] better than the day of birth." In 1 Corinthians 15:5–55, Paul wrote, "Death is swallowed up in victory. O death, where is thy sting? O grave, where is thy victory?"

In Revelation 1:18, Jesus said, "I am he that liveth, and was dead; and, behold, I am alive for evermore, Amen; and have the keys of hell and of death." After reading that, it's hard to understand how anyone calling him- or herself a Christian could possibly have any concerns about death. The One Christians believe in says He has the *keys* to hell and death. If someone who loved you said he had the keys to get you out of jail, would you worry about spending any time there?

The Koran begins by calling God merciful, and at 19:66–67 asks, "Man says: 'How is it possible, when I am dead, that I shall then be brought forth alive?' Does he not remember that We have created him once, and that he was nothing then?"

The Koran 29:64 also states, "The present life is naught but a diversion and a sport; surely the Last Abode is Life, did they but know." Did they but know, there would be no fear of death.

**Reincarnation.** According to reincarnationists, a portion of us keeps coming back again and again, living lifetime after lifetime, in body after body, until all necessary lessons are learned. How do we know when all necessary lessons have been learned? When we stop coming back.

VARIATION: We already know all there is to know, but we agreed to forget it for a specified period of time so we can take part in this great play (either opera, soap opera, horse opera, or Grand Ole Opry) called life.

If reincarnation is your belief, you, too, have nothing to fear. Death is the great liberator, a chance to take off your school clothes (or make-up) and meet with old friends at the malt shop (or corner pub) for drinks and good times.

As the Bhagavad Gita (chapter 2, verse 27), a holy text of Hindus—the largest group of reincarnationists outside Southern California—says,

> For certain is death for the born
> And certain is birth for the dead;
> Therefore over the inevitable
> Thou should not grieve.

*Death is, to us here,*
*the most terrible word we know.*
*But when we have*
*tasted its reality,*
*it will mean to us birth,*
*deliverance,*
*a new creation of ourselves.*

GEORGE MERRIMAN

Or fear.

≈

In fact, nobody really knows for sure. Many who have lived after being pronounced clinically dead report the trip to "the other side" as a pleasant journey. Almost all who remember describe roughly the same experience: looking down on their now-dead body, lifting away from earth, going through a white tunnel, being met by a loving Master form, having their life shown to them from the beginning, learning lessons from their life experiences, being given a choice to "go on" or to return and continue to "study" on earth, and choosing to go back. (Those who chose to go on, well, they are not available for comment.) Many report meeting loved ones who had previously died.

Some people remember all these events, others remember some of them, but the consistency of descriptions from a broad range of individuals—even people from *Ohio*—points to the possibility that death (or at least the transition to death) might not be so bad. (An interesting book on the subject is *Heading Toward Omega* by Kenneth Ring.)

If, as Walt Whitman put it, "Nothing can happen more beautiful than death," why don't we all just kill ourselves?

Good question—especially to ask while reading Whitman. That man seemed to have an *affair* with death. ("The sea lisped to me the low and delicious word death," "Come lovely and soothing death," "Sooner or later delicate death," "Praise! Praise! Praise! For the sure-enwinding arms of cool-enfolding death.") Yumm.

Suicide is always an option, of course. The option is, sometimes, what makes life bearable. Knowing we don't absolutely *have* to be here can make *being* here a little more bearable. I do not, however, recommend suicide.*

If, as I propose, we are here to learn, then all

---

*Exception: When you have a terminal illness and are *clearly* on the way out—almost gone, in fact—then it's between you and your Gap.

> **Arthur Dent:** *You know,*
> *it's at times like this,*
> *when I'm stuck in a Volgon air lock*
> *with a man from Betelgeuse,*
> *about to die of asphyxiation in deep space,*
> *that I really wish I'd listened to what*
> *my mother told me when I was young.*
>
> **Ford Prefect:** *Why?*
> *What did she tell you?*
>
> **Arthur:** *I don't know;*
> *I didn't listen.*
>
> THE HITCHHIKER'S GUIDE TO THE GALAXY

life—including that which is so painful it makes us want to die—can be used for learning, upliftment, and growth. Sometimes it's only after a painful process is over that we can look back and see what we learned from the situation.

In fact, we seldom know it when our greatest lessons are taking place; our experience at the time is usually confusion, pain, and/or discomfort. It's like traveling—when seeing the most exotic lands with the most amazing scenery sometimes means sleeping in tents two hundred miles from the nearest toilet. It's when we get back home, we remember the magnificent vistas. As William Burroughs explained, "There are certain things human beings are not permitted to know—like what we're doing."

Suicide is not a good idea for another reason. Before we can learn life's more advanced lessons, we must learn the basics—how to talk, walk, operate a body, read, make a living, etc. That takes *at least* twenty years. (Some people haven't mastered it in fifty.) That you're reading this book indicates you've "done your time" in the "basic" school, and are now ready for the *truly* challenging stuff. Why waste all that preparation?

Sure, "the other side" is wonderful, but you'll be spending the rest of your death there. As Malcolm Forbes had etched on his tombstone, "While alive, he lived."

While alive, live.

*When you don't have any money,*
*the problem is food.*
*When you have money it's sex.*
*When you have both it's health.*
*If everything is simply jake,*
*then you're frightened*
*of death.*

J. P. DONLEAVY

# Emergencies

There are no emergencies, only *emergences*.

Lessons don't always emerge in a methodical, orderly, systematic way. The time-frame is seldom leisurely, steady, and unhurried.

In addition to lessons, there are *tests*. Without tests, how can your Master Teachers know what you've learned, and what you need work on next?

We are, of course, tested all the time. Our successful action means we're passing tests. Walking, speaking, tying shoes—all those things that were major challenges at age two are today's often-passed tests for most of us. By merely standing up, for example, we pass gravity's ongoing tests. (Yes, gravity is a Master Teacher. So is levity.)

When we are tested in new areas, we tend to make more mistakes—it's because we haven't mastered the new area yet. That's okay. We're not *supposed* to have mastered it. We're the *student*, not the master. When the tests happen one at a time, we can usually manage them. But when the tests emerge two, three, four, fifteen at a time: emergency!

An emergency is several Master Teachers standing at once and saying, "Pop Quiz!"

When you feel yourself overwhelmed by "problems," take a look at the Master Teachers around you. See the smiling faces of Mistakes, Guilt, Resentment, Fear, Pain, Disease, Stubbornness, Addiction, Depression, Death. They're waiting to see

> *God gave burdens,*
> *also shoulders.*
>
> YIDDISH PROVERB

how well you do.

Do well. Consider them not a problem, but a challenge. Rise to the occasion.

Emerge-and-see.

Ask yourself, "What have I learned about this situation that I can use?" The answer to that question, and your successful application of it, will lead to the spontaneous emergence of achievement, fulfillment, happiness—and a gathering of justifiably proud Master Teachers.

*Oh my God!*
*I don't have a*
*quote for this page!*
*What will I do?*

*Decide what you want,*
*decide what you are willing*
*to exchange for it.*
*Establish your priorities*
*and go to work.*

H. L. HUNT

# PART FOUR

## TOOLS FOR
## SUCCESSFUL DOERS

We can learn by doing—by doing *anything*. Even if we fail—repeatedly—there's something to be learned from the failures. Of course, one of the lessons we can learn from failure is, "I want to learn some new ways of doing things so I don't have to fail so much."

Or, perhaps you already are a successful doer and, like all successful doers, you know there's always more to learn about successfully doing.

This section focuses more on "outer" achievements. The next section, "To Have Joy and to Have It More Abundantly," highlights methods for "inner" success.

You will notice, however, that most tools can be used for either inner or outer learning. The same commitment that allows you to make a million dollars can be used for achieving happiness. The same discipline that allows you to focus on your self-worth can also be used to master scuba diving.

The inner mirrors the outer. The outer mirrors the inner.

*My function in life*
*was to render clear*
*what was already*
*blindingly conspicuous.*

QUENTIN CRISP

# What Is Your Purpose?

Before taking successful action, you must first know what you want. (If you don't know what you want, how will you know when you've gotten it?) Before knowing what you want, it's good to know *why* you want it. A good way of knowing why you want it is knowing your *purpose* in life.

What is your purpose?

A purpose is something you discover. It's already there. It's always been there. You've lived your life by it—perhaps without fully realizing it. (Although when you do realize it, you'll know you've known it all along.)

It's your bellwether, your personal inner divining rod. It tells you, in any given moment, whether you're living your life "on purpose" or not.

A purpose is a simple, positive statement of why you are here. It usually begins, "I am..." and is only a few words long.

It is not a goal. A goal is something that can be reached. A purpose is a direction, like east. No matter how far east you travel, there's still lots more east to go. Purposes can be used for selecting goals, just as someone traveling east can select certain cities as guideposts along the eastward journey.

A purpose is never achieved; it is fulfilled in each moment you are "on purpose." You use your purpose to set your course in life. It's your inner compass. When you are "on course," you are "on purpose."

> *The purpose of life*
> *is a life of purpose.*
>
> ROBERT BYRNE

A purpose is not an affirmation. Affirmations are created and used to make that creation real. A purpose is not created—it is *discovered*. You already *have* a purpose. You have *always* had a purpose. It has always been the *same* purpose. Your purpose will—for the remainder of this lifetime—remain the same.

A purpose is like a heart. You don't create a heart, but, like the Tin Man in *The Wizard of Oz*, you can discover the one you've always had.

Purposes sound something like this (Don't use this list to *select* a purpose for yourself. Give yourself the time and the freedom to discover your own. These are just to give you an *idea* of what purposes sound like.): "I am a cheerful giver," "I am a happy student," "I am a devoted friend," "I serve the planet," "I am a joyful explorer," "I am a lover of life," "I want a hamburger" (all right—the last one was my *personal* goal for the moment).

There are many ways to discover your purpose. Here are a few. If one doesn't work, try another. Patience, seeker, patience! The discovery of a purpose can take a while. When you know yours, you'll know it was worth the wait.

1. Make a list of all your positive qualities. This is no time for modesty. (False humility, by the way, is just a form of egoism.) Narrow each of your good qualities to one or two words. "Loving, giving, joyful, playful, caring, effective, etc." If your list is short, ask friends for suggestions. Using these words as a starting point, find the two or three that suit you best. Arrange them in sentences starting with "I..." or "I am..." When you discover your purpose, it will "click."

2. Before going to sleep, give yourself the instruction: "When I wake up, I will know my purpose." Have pen and paper by your bed and, first thing when you wake up, write whatever words are there. It *may* be your purpose.

3. Go to your sanctuary and ask your Master Teacher. (Remember your Master Teacher?)

Once you discover your purpose, I suggest that you not tell anyone. This keeps it powerful. It also

*It is better to be hated*
*for what you are*
*than loved*
*for what you are not.*

ANDRE GIDE

keeps others from saying, "So you're a joyful giver, huh? Okay, I'll take five dollars," or "Happy helper? You don't seem very happy to *me*." Life's hard enough without having our purpose on display for the potshots of the world.

When you know your purpose, it's easier to set and achieve goals. The litmus test of any action is simply, "Does this fulfill my purpose?" If yes, you can choose whether you want to do it or not. There is—as you may already know—a certain value to being "on purpose."

*In order to be irreplaceable
one must always be different.*

COCO CHANEL

*Often people attempt*
*to live their lives backwards;*
*they try to have more things,*
*or more money,*
*in order to do more of what they want,*
*so they will be happier.*
*The way it actually works*
*is the reverse.*
*You must first be who you really are,*
*then do what you need to do,*
*in order to have what you want.*

MARGARET YOUNG

# Intention and Desire or Method and Behavior?

There are some things we want because we really want them. There are other things we want because we think they will give us what we really want. The first category I call *intentions* or *desires*. The second category I call *methods* or *behaviors*.

For example, you may say, "I want a red sports car." I may say, "Fine, and what do you want *from* the red sports car?" "I want adventure." The true desire or intention is, in fact, adventure. The red sports car was the method or behavior to get adventure.

Another example: If you say, "I want more fun," I might ask, "What can you do to have more fun?" You could then give a long list of the things you find fun to do. In this case, *fun* is the intention or desire; the enjoyable activities you've listed are your methods or behaviors for achieving fun.

A person's intentions or desires are *experiences*. They are described by words such as freedom, security, power, happiness, self-worth, success, satisfaction, respect, peace of mind, adventure, love.

The methods or behaviors people use to have these experiences are *symbols* for "the real thing." They include money, job or career, clothes, cars, house, marriage, family, sex, lovers, sex, physical appearance, sex, educational degrees, sex, and travel. (And food.)

> *One must not lose desires.*
> *They are mighty stimulants*
> *to creativeness, to love,*
> *and to long life.*

ALEXANDER BOGOMOLETZ

When people want a physical thing—and, yes, a husband, wife, child, or lover is a physical thing—they are usually talking about methods or behaviors. When they discuss inner experiences, they are generally referring to intentions or desires.

There is nothing wrong with wanting the symbols. This section, in fact, will suggest many techniques (methods? behaviors?) for getting your fair share of symbols.

It helps, however, to know that the house, car, better body, career, or money you want—yes, even a romantic relationship, religion, or spiritual path—is simply a *method* or *behavior* to get something else: something inner, something experiential (security, fun, energy, satisfaction, love, knowledge of God, inner peace).

Why does it help to know this? First, if you know the experience you're looking for, you can make whole *lists* of methods and behaviors that might fulfill it. Love can be found in more places than romantic relationships. Fun can be found without having a million dollars.

You can make a list and "scientifically" investigate it to see if a certain method or behavior fulfills a given desire or intention. If yes, fine. If no, you've still got a long list to explore.

Second, knowing the experiences you seek helps you avoid fear and disappointment. Say you *know* you want adventure and think a red sports car is the way to get it. If the car does it, fine; add "red sports car" to the list of things that (for now) work. If the car doesn't do it, that doesn't mean adventure is out of your reach. Next method or behavior, please.

Third, and perhaps most important, you learn that *you* can fulfill your own desires and intentions without too much outside help. You can fulfill your own desires or intentions *right now*. Want love? Love yourself. Want joy? Be joyful. Want adventure? The last frontier is the interior.

As you can imagine, if *you* provide *yourself* with the experiences you seek, this decreases the frantic quality of pursuing the *symbols* of life. "I can't be happy until I get..." "I won't rest until..." "My life isn't complete until I...." There's not a desire or intention we can't fulfill for ourselves, right now.

> *The last time I saw him*
> *he was walking down*
> *Lover's Lane*
> *holding his own hand.*
>
> FRED ALLEN

Ironically, once we give fully to ourselves, those symbols just seem to *cascade* in. Relationships, for example. Whom would you rather be around—a joyful, loving, happy person, or a miserable, needy, unhappy person? Well, so would everyone else. (People know this, which is why they *pretend* to be loving, happy, and joyful, in order to "catch" someone.)

When you are genuinely "up" because *you* are the source of your own "upness," people either do or do not relate to you—and whether they do or not is fine. As Frank Sinatra explains, "I bring my own crank."

You can use your behaviors and methods to discover your intentions and desires. Of each external "thing" you want, ask yourself, "What experience am I looking for?"

Experiences can be layers of an onion. Pleasure may be on the surface, but that's really a symbol for contentment, which is a symbol for peace of mind. Keep asking. Eventually you'll find experiences that are complete in and of themselves—experiences you're not using to achieve other experiences.

When you discover your fundamental desires and intentions, you'll know what you *really* want. Then, finding methods and behaviors to create the experiences is not only easier; it's more fun.

I just want to do God's will.
And He's allowed me
to go to the mountain.
And I've looked over,
and I've seen the promised land.
So I'm happy tonight.
I'm not worried
about anything.
I'm not fearing any man.

MARTIN LUTHER KING, JR.

THE NIGHT BEFORE HIS DEATH

# You Can Have Anything You Want, but You Can't Have Everything You Want

When I ask people that simple yet profound question, "What do you want?" they sometimes answer, "I want it all!" I often wonder, "If they had it all, where would they *put* it?"

There's an awful lot of "all" out there. And there's a lot more "all" to be experienced inside. The people who say they want "it all" either have not taken the time to explore what they really want, or don't realize one simple fact of life: "You can have *any*thing you want, but you can't have *every*thing you want."

Living on this planet has some down-to-earth limitations. First, we can put our body in only one place at a time. Second, there are only 24 hours a day, 365 (or 366) days per year. Third, the human lifetime is only so long (150 years seems to be tops).

The limitations become even more severe when we consider the time we spend on *maintenance*: sleeping, washing, eating—and some of us even have to make money to pay for all that.

We can't have "it all" because "all" is more than our "container" of time and space will hold.

Before you cry, "Foul!" consider: You *can* have *any*thing you want. Pick what you want most and—

> *The Wright brothers*
> *flew right through*
> *the smoke screen*
> *of impossibility.*
>
> CHARLES F. KETTERING

if it's available, if it doesn't already belong to someone else (who wants to keep it)—you can have it.

The history books are full of people who said, "I don't care if everybody thinks it's impossible, *I* think it's possible, I want it, and I'm going to get it (or do it)." And they did.

You can, too.

The catch? The more unobtainable the "want" you want, the more you must sacrifice to get it. It's not that you *can't* have it, it's that you'll have to give up many—and maybe all—other things.

I was once on a talk show and a woman called in. She said she wanted to be an actress more than anything else. She was quite upset that she hadn't succeeded yet. Our conversation went something like this:

"How much time do you spend on your career?"

"I spend *all my time.*"

"You don't sleep?"

"Of course I sleep."

"Are you in a relationship?"

"Yes, but I only see him four or five nights a week."

"Do you have a job?"

"Of course—I have to work to support my two daughters."

"How old are your daughters?"

"Four and eight."

As you can guess, this woman spent about an hour a week on her "career." What she meant to say was that she spent all of her *free time* pursuing acting. Unfortunately, it's not likely that an hour a week will give her the success she craves.

My advice to her? After establishing that she loved her daughters and loved her boyfriend and considered them more important than show biz, I suggested she be grateful for the choices she had *already made* and her successful implementation of them. I told her there were any number of successful actresses who wish they had two healthy children and a loving, romantic relationship. The acting? Make it a hobby.

The phrase "spending time" is a precise and ac-

*Who begins too much*
*accomplishes little.*

GERMAN PROVERB

curate one. We all have only so much time this time around. Spend it well.

It's as though you were in a large store (Earth). You are given enough money (time) to buy *anything* in the store, but not *everything* in the store. You can fit a lot of things in your cart (projects you start). When it comes time to pay, however, if your money runs out, that's it. And this store does not give refunds. At best, the store may reluctantly buy something back as used merchandise—at a fraction of what you paid for it.

Some people put a "want" in their cart—a new career, a relationship, a car, a house, a project—and fail to consider its cost: the time it will take to obtain *and maintain* the want.

They like to quote Edna St. Vincent Millay:

> My candle burns at both ends;
> It will not last the night;
> But, ah, my foes, and, oh, my friends—
> It gives a lovely light.

While reciting it, however, they are secretly worried about the wax dripping on the new rug—which hasn't yet been paid for. At some point, they find themselves "out of time," quoting Samuel Hoffenstein: "I burned my candle at both ends, and now have neither foes nor friends."

Some protest: "Time is money, and with money you can *buy* time." Up to a limit, that's true. But you can't hire someone to do all the things you want to do yourself (flying a plane, ballet, race car driving, reading, watching videos). And do you plan to hire people to spend time with your friends, eat your pizzas, or to entertain your lover(s)?

At a certain point in most everyone's life—rich, poor, organized, or scattered—the wants outnumber the available hours in the day. At that point, a want must go a-wanting.

The solution is preventative: choose carefully at the outset. Be grateful that, although you can't have *everything*, some very nice *anythings* await your selection.

*I'd rather have
roses on my table than
diamonds on my neck.*

EMMA GOLDMAN

# What Do You Want?

I know you know the "right" answer to this question: "I don't want a red sports car, I want adventure!" But, *really,* do you still want the sports car? That's what this chapter is about—the red sports cars of life.

In order to *get* what you want, it's very helpful to *know* what you want. If you don't know where you want to go, you probably won't get there.

The key in all this is not *what* you want, but what *you* want. When asked to list the material things they want, people often get lost in glamour: what thing can I have or do that will make me *look good?*

Glamour is a problem. It's been a problem for millions of years: "My mastodon is better than your mastodon," "My pterodactyl can fly faster than your pterodactyl." Glamour is time and energy wasted impressing others with externals.

Be true to yourself when choosing what you want. What would please *you?* If a career is more important than a relationship, say so. Just because almost every movie, popular song, and toothpaste commercial implies you'll never be a whole person until you have another to share your life, doesn't mean you have to rearrange *your* priorities. If you'd rather be *making* the movies than making whoopee, that's fine.

Conversely, if what you *really* want is a relationship and a family, but your career-oriented

> *I'd like a bird for*
> *an old lady of ninety-four.*
> *She had one,*
> *but it died*
> *and she doesn't realize it.*
> *She keeps it in a cage,*
> *talks to it,*
> *and takes it out*
> *and kisses its head.*
>
> CONTESTANT
> QUEEN FOR A DAY

friends find that hopelessly corny—tell 'em you're moving to Iowa where the corn grows tall.

I don't mean to imply that you can't have both a career and a relationship. Some can, some can't (and some in the latter category haven't realized it yet). It depends on the price of the relationship, the cost of the career, and your payments on the other items already in your cart. People often sacrifice fulfilling relationships and rewarding careers to the graven idol of glamour.

So, what do you want? Would you like a list, from one to ten? Getting that list will take pen, paper, and about an hour. Please follow each step, and please write your answers down. Even if you're *sure* you know what number one is, do you know number five? And number one *may* surprise you.

*Doing* this exercise—although it's easy—is something we tend to avoid. We intuitively know that when we choose what we want, (a) we will have to give up some "good ideas" we simply don't have time for; and (b) there's a greater chance we *will* get what we truly want (which can be scary). Some, rather than face the loss and the fear, simply accept the status quo and continue just *reading* self-help books, thank you very much.

I encourage you to set your reservations aside and do the exercise anyway.

1. Write down everything you want.* Don't worry about order, obtainability, or relative importance. As an item comes to mind, write it down. Remember, this is a list of *things*—symbols, methods, behaviors—you want. Experiences go on another list. If you want happiness, what are the things you think will bring you happiness? This is a list of things you want to have, do, and be (as in, "Be a doctor").

2. As you make your list, include what you have that you want to maintain. Your list may contain, "Maintain car, maintain house, maintain relationship."

*Using 3x5 cards makes the process easier—one "want" per card.

> *The only thing I ever dream*
> *is that I just won every*
> *beauty contest in the world*
> *and all the people I don't like*
> *are forced to build me*
> *a castle in France.*
>
> STEPHANIE VANDERKELLEN
> *NEWHART*

3. When the list is complete, set it aside and do something else—anything else. Take a walk, take a nap, eat a peach.

4. Return to the list. Did you think of any more wants during the break? Add them to the list.

5. Read the list. Cross off any wants that seem silly or trivial. If you know "Walk the dog" is not going to make your top ten, cross it off. *"Take care of* the dog," however, might—so leave that one on.

6. With your purpose in mind, read the list again. Cross off any wants that oppose your purpose. If your purpose is "I am a friend to all," then cross off "Send John a stink bomb."

If you haven't discovered your purpose yet, don't worry. Skip to number seven.

7. Classify each want into one of three categories: (A) those that are *very, very* important to you; (B) those that are *very* important to you; and (C) those that are important to you. If a want isn't important enough to make at least (C), cross it off.

8. On a clean sheet of paper, copy all your A's. If there are ten or more, stop. If there are not yet ten, copy all your B's. If there are ten or more A's plus B's, stop. If there are not ten or more A's and B's, either start over, because your list probably doesn't include all the things you want; or reclassify, because you assigned too few A's and B's.

9. With your new list (the A-B list), choose the *one thing* from that list you want *most*. Write that on a third sheet of paper. Cross that item off the A-B list. From the remaining items, pick the one that's most important. Write that on the third sheet of paper. Cross it off the A-B list. Do this eight more times. Stop.

10. You should now have ten items written on the third sheet of paper. Look at the list. Are any in *direct opposition* to any others? ("I want to stay married." "I want a divorce.") If there are, cross off the one that's the *lower* on the list. Pick another from the A-B list. That done, recopy the entire list on a clean sheet of paper. Number these one through ten.

> *Since the mind is a specific biocomputer,*
> *it needs specific instructions*
> *and directions.*
> *The reason most people*
> *never reach their goals*
> *is that they don't define them,*
> *or ever seriously consider them*
> *as believable or achievable.*
> *Winners can tell you*
> *where they are going,*
> *what they plan to do along the way,*
> *and who will be sharing the*
> *adventure with them.*
>
> DENIS WAITLEY

There's your list. This is what you want.

What about all those B's and C's? That's not the concern to focus on right now. Look at your top-ten list. Imagine enjoying each. How will you feel? What will you think? What experiences will you have when these are yours, completely and fully?

Experience that now.

*The greatest pleasure in life*
*is doing what people say*
*you cannot do.*

W ALTER B AGEHOT

*A man is not idle because
he is absorbed in thought.
There is a visible labor and
there is an invisible labor.*

VICTOR HUGO

1862

# Which Is More Powerful— the Invisible or the Visible?

Now that you have a list of the ten things you would most like, I am, of course, going to tell you to *go* get them; *get* busy; *make* them happen. *Do it!*

Later.

First, let's talk about intangibles. Pop Quiz!

**True or False: What we can see (the visible) is more powerful than what we can't see (the invisible).**

By now, you're a good enough "student" to know how to psych out the "teacher." You know that I'll probably pick something other than the obvious, logical answer. And you're right. Even if you couldn't think of an invisible thing that was more powerful than a big, strong visible thing, you still *knew* I was going to say, "Invisible is more powerful." Even if you didn't know why, you'd probably answer the Pop Quiz question False.

Is that cheating? No. That's life. That's using everything for your learning, upliftment, and growth. Congratulations! Extra points if you answered the question correctly for the "wrong" reason.

But what if I had given you an essay exam? What if you had to *explain* yourself? Quentin Crisp will now tell us how to handle that:

> If you're taking an essay exam on geography,
> and the exam could be on any of the coun-

> *We look at it*
> *and do not see it;*
> *Its name is The Invisible.*
> *We listen to it*
> *and do not hear it;*
> *Its name is The Inaudible.*
> *We touch it*
> *and do not find it;*
> *Its name is The Formless.*
>
> LAO-TZU
>
> 604–531 B.C.

tries in the world, study *one* country, and know it well. Let's say you choose China. When it comes time for the exam, and the question is, "Write one thousand words on Nigeria," you begin your essay, "Nigeria is nothing like China..." and proceed to write everything you know about China.

So if you had studied, say, Mistakes, and I asked for one thousand words on The Visible vs. The Invisible, you could begin your essay, "When talking about the visible and the invisible, it's very easy to make a mistake. A mistake, after all, is..." and write 980 additional words on mistakes.

Or, as Mark Twain once said, "Put all your eggs

in one basket and WATCH THAT BASKET!"

*Completely* invisible thus far in this chapter is any sense of direction. You may be wondering, "What *is* the point?" I thought it might be good to have a little transitional patter between the *very* material desires of your top-ten list and the undeniably immaterial ideas of the next chapter ("The Power of Thoughts").

You see, in the next chapter I plan to take you to the source, the very foundation of getting those ten things you want (and lots of others). I found this transition jarring myself, so, as a segue, I thought we'd discuss the visible and invisible for a while.

If we observe the world around us, it's easy to see that what we can't see is more powerful than what we can.

Look at air, for example. Air is hard to "look at," of course, because it's invisible. (In the places where you can see the air—such as the third level of Hades or Los Angeles—what you're seeing is pollution, not air.)

On earth, air is more powerful than almost anything. It contains oxygen for animals and carbon dioxide for plants. Without air, both would die. Air is a lifeline that is so omnipresent (it's always as close as your next breath), we take it for granted. It's essential, yet it's invisible.

"All right," some may say, "What about something physical—like a *house?* You can see a house, and if someone dropped a house on you, it would kill you faster than taking air away from you, so

> *The power of the visible*
> *is the invisible.*
>
> MARIANNE MOORE

wouldn't a house be more powerful?"

What would make the house fall? Gravity. If gravity didn't pull the house down, the house would have no power to destroy. It would just float there—like a freeze-frame from *The Wizard of Oz.*

And then there's light. You can't "see" light. It's when light reflects off something that we can see its *effects.* We can see the glow of the lightbulb, but we can't see the light traveling from the bulb to whatever it's illuminating.

If the sun radiates enough light to illuminate the earth, why is the space between here and the sun so dark? Because light waves are invisible until they strike something—namely the earth's atmosphere (which is made of our invisible friend, air; which is held in place by another invisible friend, gravity).

And heat? We can't *see* heat, but we can certainly *feel* it. If it weren't for the invisible atmosphere (air) of our planet, held in place by invisible gravity, holding invisible heat, do you know how cold the earth would be? Cold. About 280 degrees below zero at night. In summer.

Coolness is just as important for human survival—and until things approach the freezing point, coolness can't be easily perceived, either.

Can you tell the temperature of a tub of water by just looking at it? Unless it's hot enough to steam or cold enough to freeze, you probably can't. Can you tell how warm or cool a room is by seeing it through a pane of glass? Probably not.

Looking inside ourselves, we see our most powerful motivators can't be seen. Love, hate, passion, greed, fear, desire, lust, compassion, charity, goodness—all the emotions that set us in motion are invisible.

And thoughts, well, thoughts are so invisible (yes, you may be able to "see" your own thoughts, but nobody else can) and so powerful, they deserve a chapter unto themselves.

*In the province of the mind,*
*what one believes to be true*
*either is true*
*or becomes true.*

JOHN LILLY

# The Power of Thoughts

Every human achievement—from the Hoover Dam to the book you hold in your hand—began as a single thought. ("I'm gonna build a dam." "I'm gonna write a book.") Thoughts are powerful.

That single thought was, of course, followed by millions more. Some were optimistic ("Just what the world needs: another dam!" "Just what the world needs: another book!"). Some were perhaps pessimistic ("Just what the world needs: another damn book").

On the other hand, thoughts have little power at all. Without touching it, fold over the corner of this page. Think *hard* about folding over the corner of this page. Without touching it—or allowing anyone else to touch it—fold over the corner of this page. Focus all your mental strength, energy, attention, and power on folding over a corner. Either corner is fine. Just fold it over without, in any way, physically touching it.

At this point, many are inventing interesting ways to fold the corner over that fit the limitations I gave. "Maybe if I rub the book against the floor..." This demonstrates the inventiveness of the human mind—and the knowledge that unless *something* is done physically to the page, the corner is *never* going to be folded over.

If you haven't yet "given up," that's fine. You can spend as much time as you like focusing thought-power alone on folding over the corner of

> *I have found power*
> *in the mysteries of thought.*
>
> EURIPIDES
>
> 438 B.C.

this page. You can call friends. Form groups (whole movements, if you choose) dedicated to sending thoughts to fold the corner over.

Once you realize the point—that thoughts alone aren't going to do it—simply reach up and fold over the corner of this page. You don't have to even "think about it." Just—casually—reach up and fold the corner. It can be a little fold or a big fold—makes no difference.

Please do it, however.

There are other points to be made on the next page, and a folded-over corner of this page will help me make them.

Corner folded? Great.

Note the power of thoughts without action. In the physical world, seemingly little.

Note the power of the physical action alone. So powerful as to be almost effortless. Most people didn't have to work to fold over the corner of a page. It was easy. Without the power of thought to guide it, however, human physical energy is like a mindless gorilla set loose in a nuclear power plant. One can only hope the resultant damage is contained in the plant, and that certain buttons in the control room are not pushed.

When thought *and* action are combined, the results are powerful—among the most powerful forces on earth. The combination of successful communication—the sharing of thoughts—and physical action can, literally, move mountains.

If my goal were to fold over the corner of the facing page in this book, but I failed to communicate that thought to you, it's doubtful that the corner would have gotten folded over.

Consider the difficulty *I*—Peter McWilliams— would have had folding over the page in *this* book if I had to do it myself. Without your assistance, it would have been a near-insurmountable task.

I would have had to travel from wherever I was to wherever you were, gotten your attention, waited while you read to that page in the book, said, "Excuse me," picked up the book, folded over the corner, handed it back to you and said, "Thank you."

With your help, however, it was easy. All I had to

> *Thus only can you gain the secret isolated joy of the thinker, who knows that, a hundred years after he is dead and forgotten, men who never heard of him will be moving to the measure of his thought—the subtle rapture of a postponed power, which the world knows not because it has no external trappings, but which to his prophetic vision is more real than that which commands an army.*
>
> OLIVER WENDELL HOLMES, JR.
>
> 1886

do was write a few sentences. All you had to do was reach up and fold over the corner. A *successfully communicated thought*, from one human mind to another, is one of the most powerful forces I know.

Does it always work? Nah. You can successfully communicate a thought, and the other person can do nothing about it. You can successfully communicate a thought, and the other person may do just the opposite.

But when it does work, ah, there is power, grace, and magic.

*Courage is the price that life exacts*
*for granting peace.*
*The soul that knows it not,*
*knows no release*
*From little things;*
*Knows not the livid*
*loneliness of fear,*
*Nor mountain heights where bitter joy*
*can hear*
*The sound of wings.*

AMELIA EARHART

*Baseball is fun*
*for you & me.*

*There is batting and fielding*
*and making an out,*

*There is doubles & triples*
*and even home runs,*

*But what I like about*
*baseball is for the fun.*

MATT BOHN

AT AGE 11

# Fielding Your Dreams

How powerful are thoughts that become dreams? Here is an example.

A writer, W. P. Kinsella, sat in Calgary, Canada, and had a thought: what if an Iowa corn farmer had a dream, and, combining that dream with action, he was able to reunite with his father, who had died many years earlier, for a game of baseball?

Kinsella did something about his dream. He wrote a novel called *Shoeless Joe*. The book was read by film director Phil Alden Robinson. Without their ever meeting, the dream (thought) was passed (successfully communicated). Robinson's dream was to write and direct a film based on the book. His dream, too, was for Kevin Costner to play the farmer who converts some of his farmland into a baseball field.

He successfully communicated his dream to Costner, who helped pass the dream along to some money-people in Hollywood. Many successfully communicated dreams later, a film was made— *Field of Dreams*.

It was (and is) a great film, a great success (Hollywood translation: it made a lot of money), and an Academy Award nominee.

Well and good. But the power of that dream didn't end there.

The farm on which the film was shot is owned by Don Lansing. Since the film's opening, thousands of people—moved by the power of a

> *It's not just my parents*
> *who believe they'll see*
> *Matt on the field, it's me too.*
> *I'll see Matt through my heart.*
> *You have to believe before you*
> *can see things on the field,*
> *and if you believe, you'll see.*

STEPHANIE BOHN

AT AGE 9

dream—have traveled to Dyersville, Iowa, to see the field, play a little baseball, get married (really, at home plate)—but mostly to affirm that dreams can, and do, come true.

But the story is *still* not over.

(If you haven't seen the film, now is a wonderful time to set down the book, go rent the video, watch it, and return to this spot for the conclusion of this story.)

Here is a letter Lansing received in the fall of 1989:

Dear Don,

You don't know me; my name is Jim Bohn. My son

Matt and mother-in-law Lena Blaha died in the crash of United Airlines Flight 232 in Sioux City on July 19.

This past spring I had taken my son and family to see the movie "Field of Dreams." We loved the movie. I had no idea that the "field" was still there. I figured that after the filming it had been re-planted. To my surprise and delight, I read an article last evening in our Pittsburgh (PA.) Press newspaper that you have been maintaining the field. How long do you plan to maintain it as the baseball field? Will you still receive visitors next summer? We are planning to visit Sioux City next summer for the anniversary of the crash and would love to stop and visit the field.

Matt was 12 and loved baseball. So do I, as my father before me did. I've always coached Matt's team. For the past 6 years we have had a great time enjoying each other and baseball.

As you may know the plane crashed in an Iowa corn field. I found the whole idea very ironic; the story of an Iowa corn farmer who plows up his corn field to make a baseball field where dreams come true and my son, who loved baseball, dying in an Iowa corn field. My dreams came to an end.

When I was in Sioux City after the crash, I stayed at Briar Cliff College. From my room the most prominent object in the landscape was a baseball field. I could not stop thinking about the movie, the crash and a corn field in Iowa. There was message there.

When I read the article last evening I knew I had to visit the "field." Please let me know of your plans

> *I was able to read your letter.*
> *If the movie means*
> *anything to me now*
> *it's that you get that chance to*
> *walk with your son.*
> *I am with you in spirit.*
> *Love, Kevin.*
>
> KEVIN COSTNER

for the field. I hope I will have the chance to walk with my son one more time.

A single thought, by a writer living in Canada, became a dream inspiring millions, and gave comfort to a family in Pittsburgh, Pennsylvania. Thus, the power of a dream.*

---

*Jim, Cindy, and Stephanie Bohn honored me by allowing me to join them on the field in July of 1990. It was a beautiful, healing day. For me, it was a dream come true. And the dream continues.

> *It does not matter*
> *how slowly you go*
> *so long as you do not stop.*
>
> CONFUCIUS

UPDATE: As it turned out, I rewrote this chapter only two days after the September 1994 USAir crash en route to Pittsburgh. I called Jim, Cindy, and Stephanie (who will be fourteen in three weeks). They told me that although the recent tragedy brought back painful memories, they have nevertheless volunteered to help some of the families devastated by the crash. The dream—the gift, and life—goes on.

*When people say to me:*
*"How do you do so many things?"*
*I often answer them,*
*without meaning to be cruel:*
*"How do you do so little?"*
*It seems to me that people*
*have vast potential.*
*Most people can do extraordinary things*
*if they have the confidence*
*or take the risks.*
*Yet most people don't.*
*They sit in front of the telly and*
*treat life as if it goes on forever.*

PHILIP ADAMS

# The Thought-Feeling-Action Pyramid

Successful achievement requires the use and co-ordination of thoughts, feelings, and actions. They form the three sides of a triangle—a pyramid.

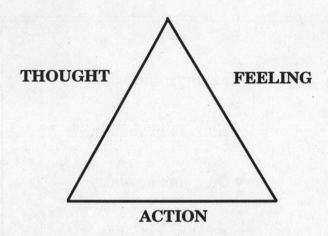

Like a stool that requires at least three legs for stability, ongoing accomplishment requires thoughts, feelings, and actions for success.

**Thoughts** spark the process, get it going. **Feelings** keep the thoughts alive, encourage similar thoughts, and get the body moving. **Action** is important to accomplish the physical tasks necessary for achievement.

Without all three, the pyramid collapses.

*To change one's life:*

- *Start immediately.*

- *Do it flamboyantly.*

- *No exceptions.*

WILLIAM JAMES

# Commitment

One of the most powerful tools in the achievement tool kit is the combination of commitment and action.

W. H. Murray, in *The Scottish Himalayan Expedition,* explained it:

> Until one is committed, there is hesitancy, the chance to draw back, always ineffectiveness. Concerning all acts of initiative (and creation) there is one elementary truth, the ignorance of which kills countless ideas and splendid plans: that *the moment one definitely commits oneself, then Providence moves too.* All sorts of things occur to help one that would never otherwise have occurred. A whole stream of events issues from the decision, raising in one's favor all manner of unforeseen incidents and meetings and material assistance, which no man could have dreamed would have come his way. I have learned a deep respect for one of Goethe's couplets:
>
> > *Whatever you can do,*
> > *or dream you can, begin it.*
> > *Boldness has genius,*
> > *power and magic in it.*

When you're so committed to something you *know* it's going to happen, you act as though it's going to happen. That action is a powerful affirmation.

> *The great aim of education
> is not knowledge
> but action.*
>
> HERBERT SPENCER

If you sit back and *say* you're committed, but wait for conclusive proof before you act, little is likely to happen. It's called "playing it safe." I don't recommend that game. Not only is it ineffective and demoralizing, it's already being played by people who are absolute *masters* at it. The field, in fact, is overcrowded. You'll have to study long and hard to beat them at that game.

Be bold. Commit and act. Your action indicates the depth of your commitment. Action can also determine the measure of support you'll get from others.

If you tell friends, "I'm going to visit Hawaii, someday," they'll probably say, "That's nice."

If you tell them, however, while heading for the door, suitcase in hand, a nonrefundable ticket in the pocket of your funny-looking flowered shirt, your friends are more likely to say, "Can we drive you to the airport? Do you need anything? Can we help you carry your lei?"

What is your purpose? Commit to it.

What experiences do you want? Commit to giving yourself those experiences regularly.

Look at your top-ten list. Commit to each goal.

You are, in fact, not committing to any *project*. You are committing to yourself.

*Never esteem anything*
*as of advantage to you*
*that will*
*make you break your word*
*or lose your self-respect.*

MARCUS AURELIUS ANTONINUS

121–180 A.D.

# Your Word and How to Keep It

Your word is one of the most precious things you own. Do not give it lightly. Once given, do everything within your power not to break it. A broken word, like a broken cup, cannot hold very much for very long.

Does *one* broken agreement matter? One broken agreement is like a grain of sand. To a lake, one grain of sand is nothing. Gather enough grains of sand, however, and a lake becomes a swamp. Add enough more, and it becomes a bog. (Ever feel bogged down?) Add enough more, and it becomes a desert. (Did you ever feel barren inside? Did you ever plant a dream and wonder why it did not grow?)

No, one grain of sand doesn't much matter (unless, of course, the winds of fate blow it back in your eye). Gather enough grains day after day for a lifetime, and your only effective action might be sandbagging.*

Most of us look back on a seemingly endless

---

*If you found that last analogy heavy-handed, you should see the ones I discarded: your life might not mature beyond the sandbox; you may find yourself caught in a sand trap; if you break agreements with others, expect to get sandblasted; if you don't keep written agreements, they could turn into sandpaper; if you learn to swiftly sidestep agreements, you'll have quicksand; you may be visited by a wicked sand witch—they went on and on.

> *I phoned my dad to tell him*
> *I had stopped smoking.*
> *He called me a quitter.*
>
> STEVEN PEARL

trail of broken agreements. That's a lot of sand. Is it, then, hopeless? Not at all. Declare your past broken agreements a *beach,* and get on with your life. (The techniques given in the chapters "For Giving" and "For Getting" are especially useful, as is the exercise in "Heal the Past.")

If our word is so important, what (or who) would keep us from keeping it? Once again, I present a familiar cast of characters: rebels, the unconscious, comfort junkies, and approval seekers. (By the way, don't get too down on this unworthiness tribe; the Master Teachers employ them as Master Testers. They're friends, too.)

**Rebels** will break a rule just because it's a rule.

"Rules are for fools!" they claim. They consider agreements of any kind—including ones they make, involving things they want to do—rules. They claim they have no commitments in life—only options.

**The Unconscious** use the excuse, "I forgot!" whenever an agreement is broken (which is often). If they genuinely *did* forget, they consider that a sufficient explanation. When asked, "Why didn't you write it down," the unconscious may say, "I meant to, but I forgot." They misplaced their date-book. Where? You know the answer to that one.

**Comfort Junkies** will keep agreements—if they want to at the moment. If it means doing something uncomfortable, however, they don't do it. This is most of the time. To make an agreement is easy. (It's less uncomfortable than saying no.) To actually *do* something when the time arrives is not comfortable. Calling and saying they won't be there is uncomfortable, too, so they avoid the whole situation.

**Approval Seekers** will agree to do something because, when they do, they get approval. Their schedules become hopelessly overcrowded, so keeping all those conflicting agreements becomes impossible. Their reasons for breaking agreements are excellent ones, however: visiting the sick, feeding the homeless, feeding pet butterflies (I tried it; it worked)—designed to get approval even while breaking an agreement.

How to keep agreements? A few suggestions:

**1. Make only agreements you plan to keep.**

> *One must have*
> *a good memory*
> *to be able to keep*
> *the promises one makes.*
>
> NIETZSCHE

Learn to say no, or maybe, or I'll get back to you (and *do* get back to them). If you don't want to do *now* whatever it is you're agreeing to do *later,* you probably won't want to do it when the time comes, so make your "no" known now.

2. **Make every agreement important.** Some play the game, "This agreement is more important than that agreement." In terms of ramifications "out there," that may be true, but inside yourself, each time you break your word, no matter how seemingly trivial, it costs.

3. **Keep the agreements you've made.** Even if

keeping an agreement is uncomfortable, out-
rageously expensive, or in some way seemingly prohibitive—keep it anyway. Doing this
may show you—experientially—the wisdom
of suggestion #1. Slip-sliding out of agreements at the last minute will only show you
that you know how to slip-slide out of agreements at the last minute. Most of us already
know how to do that fairly well.

4. **Write agreements down.** Keep a calendar or
   datebook. Record your agreements. Review
   the calendar at least once a day.

5. **Communicate.** If a conflict arises and you
   may have to rearrange an agreement, communicate as soon as you discover the conflict.
   There are at least two ways to reschedule an
   agreement: "Something more important
   than keeping my agreement with you has
   come up, so let's reschedule," or, "We have
   an agreement, and I'm willing to keep it, but
   I'd really appreciate it if we could move it to
   another time." Which do you suppose is
   more accountable, courteous, and recommended? (By the way, if you use the second
   approach, don't do it as a technique—mean
   it. If the other person says, "I want you to
   keep your agreement anyway," be prepared
   to keep it.)

When you lovingly keep your word—keep it
safe, keep it strong, keep it true—you will know the
power of it. When you lend it to a cause—espe-

> *His word burned*
> *like a lamp.*
>
> ECCLESIASTICUS
>
> 48:1

cially one of your own choosing—its effect will be powerful. Its effect will be known.

*The price of greatness*
*is responsibility.*

SIR WINSTON CHURCHILL

*For the very true
beginning of wisdom
is the desire of discipline;
and the care of discipline
is love.*

WISDOM OF SOLOMON

6:17

# Discipline

Most of us associate the word *discipline* with punishment of a precise and exacting nature—fourth-grade teachers and the military are notorious for discipline. To call someone a disciplinarian is seldom a compliment.

To call someone Machiavellian is usually not nice, either. Maybe it was Machiavelli who gave discipline a bad name. In 1532 he wrote,

> A prince should therefore have no other aim or thought but war and discipline, for that is the only art that is necessary to one who commands.

The word *discipline* comes from two very nice words: *discipulus*, meaning pupil, and *discere*, to learn. Discipline, then, is devotion to learning.

I like to think of discipline not as forcing yourself to do *without* (the austerity school), but as keeping your attention focused on what you *want*.

When your attention is focused on what you want, the emotions and body tend to follow. Our attention is like a flashlight beam in a dark room. What we focus the beam on, we emotionally respond to, and move our body accordingly. As Schiller wrote in 1799, "The eye sees the open heaven, / The heart is intoxicated with bliss."

For example, are you content reading this book? If so, that's the thing to focus on. You could, if you wanted to feel deprived, think about *everything else in the entire world* you *could* be doing *right now* ex-

> *Liberty is a beloved discipline.*
>
> GEORGE C. HOMANS

cept that you are *sacrificing all those incredible experiences* to sit and read this book. But this book is supposed to be *good for you,* so keep sitting here reading it, *no matter how much you want to do all those other wonderful things.*

This is how many people view discipline. My suggestion? Focus on what you're doing. If what you're doing at the moment is not entirely pleasing (I don't mean *this* moment with *this* book, of course; I mean *some other* moment with *some other* book), ask yourself, "Does what I'm doing lead to something that *is* pleasing?" If yes, then focus on the pleasant goal. If no, do something else.

That's being a disciple.

*Unified, disciplined,*
*armed with the secret powers of the atom*
*and with knowledge*
*as yet beyond dreaming,*
*Life, forever dying to be born afresh,*
*forever young and eager,*
*will presently stand upon this earth*
*as upon a footstool*
*and stretch out its realm*
*amidst the stars.*

H. G. WELLS

1920

**Beaver:** *Gee, there's something wrong with just about everything, isn't there Dad?*

**Ward:** *Just about, Beav.*

# Positive Focusing

Ever wonder why it's so difficult to keep negative thoughts out of your mind for any period of time? Ever berate yourself for not being able to hold a more positive thought longer? There's no need for self-reproach; the odds are so stacked against us, the fact that we have *any* positive thought *at all* is something of a miracle.

Here's what we're up against:

1. **The Fight or Flight Response.** This is an inbuilt, physiological response to danger. When danger is perceived (not actually happening, mind you, just *perceived)* the body reacts. The body calls an All Alert and prepares to either fight or flee *for its life.*

   This was a very handy response for millions of years, but today, for most of us, it's counterproductive. (If you are a police officer, a firefighter, or make your living as a contestant on television game shows, the Fight or Flight Response may still come in handy.)

   Part of the Fight or Flight Response is focusing the mind on *what's wrong* in the environment. This was helpful in the days when humans had to find the saber-tooth tigers before the tigers found them. Today, this intense, life-or-death searching for "What's wrong?" usually unearths *something* that's not right. That "something" may trigger another round of the Fight or Flight Response. The

> *Nobody, as long as he*
> *moves about among the*
> *chaotic currents of life,*
> *is without trouble.*
>
> CARL JUNG

truly bad news? All of this negative-fact finding is *completely* automatic.

2. **Childhood programming.** As I've mentioned before, our parents, often, trained us by telling us what *not* to do. All the things we did correctly—and there were many—were quickly accepted (and then expected) as "normal" behavior. Our occasional departures from our parents' Ideal Child Behavioral Matrix? The boom lowered. (You can skip this point if your parents were the kind who smiled and said, "Isn't that sweet? What remarkable individuality you're showing, dear, by pouring honey on the cat!") Is it any won-

der, even today, we sometimes find ourselves unconsciously scanning the environment, looking for *bad* things *not* to do?

3. **The general negativity around us.** We turn on the news, and what's the news? *Bad* news. We pick up the newspaper and what do we read? News of fresh disasters. Commercials warn us of bad breath, body odor, constipation, how it feels when a sesame seed gets caught under dentures.

   The favorite conversation? Gossip. The favorite activity? Complaining. Between 4:00 and 7:00 p.m., in cocktail lounges all over town, the citizenry gathers for the daily meeting of the Ain't-It-Awful Club. For the price of a drink (and you get two-for-one), you can tell your day's troubles to a stranger—providing you are willing to listen for an equal length of time to the stranger's woes. For some unknown reason, this is called The Happy Hour.

4. **Everything's falling apart (entropy).** How do you like this entropy law? Everything is in a state of deterioration. Leave something alone, and it rots. We know that, but do we need a mathematical formula to tell us how fast? Entropy comes from a Greek word meaning transformation. What they really mean is that everything is transforming into something *worse*.

5. **Genetics.** Well, there's nothing much we can

> *The only reason*
> *I would take up jogging*
> *is so that I could hear*
> *heavy breathing again.*
>
> ERMA BOMBECK

do about *that*, now is there? Hopeless.

All of this internal and external programming will, naturally, lead to negative thoughts. *No big deal.* Really. Let them drift through your mind like leaves on a patio. There's no need to resist them, hold onto them, or entertain them (I'm talking about thoughts here, not leaves).

What's important is your *focus*. Where—in the big picture—are you putting your attention? If you're focused on your *goal*, you can have any number of positive and negative thoughts along the way. (And probably will.)

It's a journey. As long as you keep moving toward your destination, you're doing fine. It's when you stop moving, or are not moving toward your destination, that some "course correction" is in order.

Those who enjoy being on the train, and those who do not enjoy being on the train, get to the same destination at the same time. Yes, there are things you can do to enjoy the train more. Lots of techniques for enjoyment are given in the next section (Part Five). For now, however, know that being on the train that's going in the direction of your choice is all it takes.

Naturally, the more positive thoughts you have, the more positive you'll feel. If you want to feel happy, think about happy things. An unending stream of "happy thoughts" is not, however, necessary to reach your goal.

*Motion* and *direction* are.

*The words "I am..."*
*are potent words;*
*be careful what*
*you hitch them to.*
*The thing you're claiming*
*has a way of reaching back*
*and claiming you.*

A. L. KITSELMAN

# Affirmations

*Affirm* means to make firm, solid, more real. Thoughts—not very solid—when repeated over and over, become more and more firm. They become feelings, behaviors, methods, experiences, and things. What we think about, we can become.

We affirm all the time. Sometimes we affirm negatively; sometimes we affirm positively. In the words of Henry Ford, "If you think you can do a thing, or think you can't do a thing; you're right."

I, of course, am going to suggest that you consciously affirm the positive. Many of us already have the unconscious habit of affirming the negative. To change that, I quote Johnny Mercer, "You've got to accentuate the positive, eliminate the negative, latch on to the affirmative."

Affirmations often begin with "I am...." "I am a happy, healthy, wealthy person." "I am joyful no matter what is happening around me." "I am loving and kind." If you're affirming for material things, it's a good idea to start even those with "I am...." "I am enjoying my new house." "I am creative and content in my new career."

Affirmations are best expressed in the present. "I want a new car," affirms *wanting* a new car. If what you want is *wanting* a new car, then that's a good affirmation. What you probably want, however, is the *car.* "I am safely and happily enjoying my beautiful new car." Affirm as though you already have what you want, even though you don't yet have it.

> *I'd love to see*
> *Christ come back*
> *to crush the spirit of hate*
> *and make men*
> *put down their guns.*
> *I'd also like just one more*
> *hit single.*
>
> TINY TIM

(The operative word is "yet.")

No matter how "impossible" something may seem, put it into an affirmation and give it a try. Say it, out loud, at least one hundred times before you decide how "impossible" something might be. After one hundred repetitions, you may find yourself quite comfortable with the idea.

You can write affirmations on paper and put them in places you will see them often—on the bathroom mirror, refrigerator, next to your bed, on the car dashboard. You can also record them on endless-loop cassette tapes and play them in the background all day (and night).

A powerful technique is to say your affirmation

while looking into your eyes in a mirror. All your limitations about the thing you're affirming are likely to surface, but persevere. Outlast the negative voices. Plant the seed of your affirmation deep.

Your purpose is already an affirmation. Say it to yourself often. Create affirmations for each of the experiences you want. They can be very simple: "I am content." "I am joyful and calm in the peace of my mind." "I am feeling love." "I am strong and powerful." Also, write several affirmations for each item on your top-ten list.

Affirmations work if you use them. The more you use them, the more they work. They can be used anywhere, anytime, while doing almost anything.

It's a good idea to end all your affirmations with "...this or something better, for the highest good of all concerned."

The "...this or something better..." lets ten million come in when you merely asked for a million, and "...for the highest good of all concerned" assures that your affirmation is fulfilled in a way that's best for everyone.

Learn to automatically turn all your wishes and wants into affirmations. Then start catching your negative thoughts, switching them around, and making affirmations out of them. By only slightly revising the negative chatter (changing "can't" to "can," "won't" to "will," "hate" to "love," etc.), you can turn all those formerly limiting voices into a staff of in-house affirmation writers.

> *Affirmation of life*
> *is the spiritual act*
> *by which man ceases*
> *to live unreflectively*
> *and begins to devote himself*
> *to his life with reverence*
> *in order to raise it*
> *to its true value.*
> *To affirm life is to deepen,*
> *to make more inward,*
> *and to exalt the will to live.*
>
> ALBERT SCHWEITZER

Here are a few to get you started, but this is a very brief list.

- "I am feeling warm and loving toward myself."

- "I am worthy of all the good in my life."

- "I am one with the Universe, and I have more than I need."

- "I am happy that I always do the best I can with what I know and always use everything for my advancement."

- "I am forgiving myself unconditionally."

- "I am grateful for my life."

- "I am loving and accepting myself and others."

- "I am treating all problems as opportunities to grow in wisdom and love."

- "I am relaxed, trusting in a higher plan that's unfolding for me."

- "I am automatically and joyfully focusing on the positive."

- "I am giving myself permission to live, love, and laugh."

- "I am creating and singing affirmations to create a joyful, abundant, fulfilling life."

- "...this or something better for the highest good of all concerned."

*It's no good running*
*a pig farm badly*
*for thirty years while saying,*
*"Really I was meant to be*
*a ballet dancer."*
*By that time,*
*pigs will be your style.*

QUENTIN CRISP

# Effectiveness vs. Efficiency

The best comparison between effectiveness and efficiency I've heard is this: Efficiency is getting the job done *right*. Effectiveness is getting the *right job done*.

People who excel in life—the so-called "winners"—don't do twice as much or five times as much or a hundred times as much as "average" people. Winners, it has been shown, only do *a few percentage points more* than everybody else.

The winner of a two-hour marathon need only be a few seconds ahead of all the other runners to win. First, second, and third place winners can all come in within a minute of each other. The 20,000 other runners are simply numbers.

In business, the winners often make only five more phone calls per day than average or read five more journals per month or get five more good ideas per year.

But it's not *volume* or *speed* I'm necessarily talking about. In athletic competition, as in life, it's not *how many* events you win, but *which ones* that determine the champions.

Some explain this distinction with what's called the 80/20 theory: 80% of your effort produces 20% of your results, and 20% of your effort produces the other 80% of your results.

The theory claims that you spend 80% of your time wearing 20% of your clothes, and 20% of your time wearing 80% of your clothes; you spend 80%

> *I take my children everywhere,*
> *but they always find*
> *their way back home.*
>
> ROBERT ORBEN

of your time with 20% of your friends, and 20% of your time with 80% of your friends; you spend 80% of your career resources producing 20% of your results, and 20% of your resources producing 80% of your results; and so on.

These aren't precise figures, of course. They do, however, show that *effort* and *results* are not necessarily in direct proportion—not even close, in fact.

If the 80/20 theory is even partially true, imagine what would happen if you started taking time and resources from the less effective 80% activities and moved them to the highly effective 20% activities. One percent more *effective* action would produce 5% more results.

How can you tell the 20% more effective action from the other 80%? Watch. Look. Listen. "I keep six honest serving men / (They taught me all I knew); / Their names are What and Why and When / And How and Where and Who" (Rudyard Kipling). Keep track of what you do and the results it produces.

You'll notice patterns emerging. "I spend as much time doing A as doing B, but B produces twice as many results." When you notice that, take a little time from A and give it to B. See what happens. You will probably get less from A, but do you get proportionately more from B?

Here's my nursery rhyme for today (if it's good enough for Rudyard Kipling...): "Life's experiments are great fun. / This is but another one."

*While one person hesitates*
*because he feels inferior,*
*the other is busy*
*making mistakes and*
*becoming superior.*

HENRY C. LINK

# It's Not That People Plan to Fail, They Just Fail to Plan

Here is the truth about making a plan: The plan itself never works. If, however, you *do* make a plan, the chances of getting what you want significantly increase.

Let's say you made a plan to do something. You broke your goal into action steps, and estimated the amount of time each step would take. The plan called for step A to take one week, step B to take two weeks, step C to take one week, step D to take a month, and step E to take a day. This would lead you to F, which is what you want.

When you get to F, however, you may look back on your original plan with amusement: Almost nothing went "according to plan." Step A took only a day. Step B took a week. Step C, as it turned out, had five subsets, taking two weeks *each*. When you got to step D, you discovered that nobody did step D anymore. Step E took ten minutes.

Without the faulty plan, however, you might never have ventured forth to learn all you needed to know to get to F. F is where you wanted to go; F is where you got. You just didn't get there the way you had planned. So, even though it's probably not going to be accurate, make a plan anyway.

If you don't already have one, get a date book of some kind with room for daily planning. Then

> *Zeus does not bring*
> *all men's plans*
> *to fulfillment.*
>
> HOMER

start laying out your step-by-step progression to accomplish each goal on your top-ten list. I strongly
suggest you plan *at least* one activity to move toward *each* of your top ten *each week.*

Why?

Ready for a hard truth? *If you're not actively involved in getting what you want, you don't really want
it.*

People kid themselves for years—decades,
sometimes—with a goal that, in fact, they don't really want. How do I know they didn't want it? Because they never really did anything to get it. If they
really wanted it, they would have, over the years,
consistently done something to get it.

People look back and say, "I coulda been..." or "I coulda had...." Maybe, but they also "coulda" done more to obtain it. I don't want you to face a case of the coulda's. Please do something about each item on your top-ten list every week.

After a few months of doing something each week, you may discover you don't want one of your goals after all. Without the action, however, you might not have known it. If you decide you don't want it, a slot in your top-ten list has just opened up.

If you're scheduling things *not* related to your top-ten list, and finding you "don't have time" for things on your top-ten list, I suggest you either (a) rearrange your top-ten list, or (b) rearrange your schedule.

Break each of your top-ten goals into *next doable steps*. A doable step is something you can actually do. "Learn to use a computer," is too vague. "Call friends who have a computer and ask the best way to learn to use a computer," is a doable step. You can schedule that one—give it a date, time, and duration. (April 16, 4:00 p.m., two hours.) If you can't assign it a date, time, and duration, there's probably a more doable next step available.

Then start writing these steps in your date book. Schedule your time. Budget your time as you would budget your money. Use a pencil, as you're apt to make changes, but do commit to the steps you put in your book. Be flexible, of course. This is meant to be a spur to action, not a hog-tie.

For the next few weeks, plan hour by hour. The

> *We can act*
> *as if there were a God;*
> *feel as if we were free;*
> *consider Nature as if she*
> *were full of special designs;*
> *lay plans as if we*
> *were to be immortal;*
> *and we find then*
> *that these words*
> *do make a genuine difference*
> *in our moral life.*
>
> WILLIAM JAMES

next month, day by day. The months after that, week by week. When you project a project to completion, pick another and start scheduling that.

Sitting with the days of your life before you—all the time you have to spend on *everything*—and allocating time can be confusing, exhilarating, painful, exciting, and fearful.

But please do it. One thing's for sure: you'll spend that time doing *something*. The only question is: do you want to control your time, or do you want your time to control you?

*Make no little plans;*
*they have no magic*
*to stir men's blood.*

DANIEL HUDSON BURNHAM

*You said, "but."*
*I've put my finger on the whole trouble.*
*You're a "but" man.*
*Don't say, "but."*
*That little word "but" is the difference*
*between success and failure.*
*Henry Ford said,*
*"I'm going to invent the automobile,"*
*and Arthur T. Flanken said,*
*"But…"*

SGT. ERNIE BILKO
THE PHIL SILVERS SHOW

# Get Off Your Buts!

You know what life is for; you know what your limitations are; you know the true identity of your Master Teachers; you have tools, tools, and more tools; you know what you want; you've planned it out—all right—ready, set...

Do it!

When the time comes to *do it,* panic descends.

The unworthiness warriors march out in full regalia. Rebellion says, "But why should I do it *his* way? I'll do it *my way* in *my own time.*" Unconsciousness stumbles forward and says, "But this is all too much to keep track of." The approval seeker compliments me on the book's cover, but claims to be already overcommitted.

In situations of action vs. status quo, however, one of the unworthiness tribe stands head and shoulders above the rest: the comfort junkie.

Consider this: people have precisely what they want in their lives—not what they *think* they want, but what they *actually want.*

What we have is based on moment-to-moment choices of what we *do.* In each of those moments, we choose. We either take a risk and move toward what we want, or we play it safe and choose comfort.

Most of the people, most of the time, choose comfort. In the end, people either have excuses or experiences; reasons or results; buts or brilliance; they either have what they wanted, or they have a

> *Victory belongs to*
> *the most persevering.*
>
> NAPOLEON

detailed list of all the reasons why not (rationalize = rational lies).

Almost all excuses and reasons are motivated by fear—fear of fatigue, fear of not doing it perfectly, fear of looking foolish, fear of mistakes, fear of losing, fear of being let down, fear of facing unworthiness, fear of getting angry; in short, fear that we might be uncomfortable.

We tell ourselves, "I won't do this now; I'm too tired, *but* I'll do it tomorrow when I can make a fresh start." The next morning, "I'm not in the mood, *but* I'll do it this afternoon." Come afternoon, there's some other "important" activity. Our original "plan" is postponed till evening, when friends just happen to stop over, *but* everything is put off until the following morning—*but* again.

The reasons for the postponements, by the way, are not always unpleasant. Sometimes they are the most wonderful, positive "opportunities" imaginable: a party, a trip, a dinner, friends, relationships, "easy money," and so on.

I call them all—positive or negative—the same thing: distractions. If they're not definite steps on the way to *your* goals, they're distractions.

When a distraction arises, ask yourself: would you rather have the distraction, or would you rather have your goal? It's tough to see it that way, because the goal of, say, writing a book may mean an entire evening spent researching a dull but important detail. This research cannot compare to the fun of the party to which you've just been invited.

The right question to ask yourself is: which is more *important,* the party or the book? *Not:* which is more appealing at this moment, the party or the dull research? After a thousand choices—distraction vs. work—you will have either (a) an extensive collection of party favors, or (b) a book.

These choices are made daily, hourly, moment-by-moment.

If you want to achieve more, declare your reasons unreasonable, your excuses inexcusable—and get off your buts!

In Endymion, I leaped
headlong into the sea,
and thereby have
become better acquainted
with the soundings,
the quicksands, and the rocks,
than if I had stayed upon
the green shore,
and piped a silly pipe,
and took tea and comfortable advice.

JOHN KEATS

1818

# The Comfort Zone

We all live within the comfort zone. It's the arena of activities we have done often enough to feel comfortable doing again. For most, this includes walking, talking, driving, spending time with friends, making money in certain ways—all those once-difficult and fearful things that we now find easy and comfortable.

Imagine the comfort zone as a circle: Inside the circle are those things we are comfortable doing; outside is everything else. The wall of the circle is not, alas, a wall of protection. It is a wall of fear; a wall of limitation.

The *illusion* is that the wall keeps us from bad things and keeps bad things from us. In reality, the bad things get in just fine (perhaps you've noticed). In reality, too, the wall prevents us from getting what we want.

When we do something new, something different, we push against the parameters of our comfort zone. If we do the new thing often enough, we overcome the fear, guilt, unworthiness, hurt feelings, and anger, and our comfort zone expands. If we back off and honor the limitation, our comfort zone shrinks. It's a dynamic, living thing, always expanding or contracting.

When our comfort zone expands in one area, it expands in other areas as well. When we succeed at something, our confidence and self-esteem increase, and we take that confidence and self-esteem

> *Life is either*
> *a daring adventure*
> *or nothing.*
> *Security does not exist in nature,*
> *nor do the children of men*
> *as a whole experience it.*
> *Avoiding danger is no safer*
> *in the long run than exposure.*
>
> HELEN KELLER

with us into other endeavors.

When we "give in" to our comfort zone, the zone contracts. Our belief that we "aren't strong enough," "can't do it" and are, basically, "not good enough" often prevents us from even *thinking* about approaching "the wall" again for some time.

For some, the comfort zone shrinks to the size of their apartment: they never leave home without anxiety; some people never leave home at all. They sit and watch the news on TV. The news certainly supports the notion that it's a hostile, dangerous place out there, and it's better to stay home.

For a few, the comfort zone shrinks to a space smaller than their own body. We've all probably seen or heard of institutionalized people who are afraid to move any part of their body in any direction. That is when the comfort zone "wins" its greatest victory.

That and suicide. The "it" some people refer to when they "just can't take it anymore" is the need to *constantly* be confronting the fear of leaving the comfort zone just to keep the fear at bay.

Here is one of the great ironies of life: Those who are doing what they want to do and are consciously expanding their comfort zone at every opportunity experience *no more fear* than people who are passively trying to keep life "as comfortable as possible."

Fear is a part of life. Some people feel fear when they press against their comfort zone and make it larger. Other people feel fear when they even *think* they *might* do something that gets them even *close* to the (ever-shrinking, in their case) boundary of their comfort zone. *Both feel the same fear.*

In fact, people in shrinking comfort zones probably feel more fear. They not only feel fear; they also feel the fear of feeling fear; and the fear of the fear of feeling fear; and on and on. The person who develops the habit of moving through fear when it appears, feels it only once. It's the old "A coward dies a thousand deaths, a brave man dies but one."

Some people don't just honor their comfort zone, they *worship* it. When they feel fear, they think it is God saying to them, personally and directly, "Don't do this." Some have, in fact, found scriptural references to support their inaction. Not

> *A coward dies*
> *a hundred deaths,*
> *a brave man only once...*
> *But then, once is enough,*
> *isn't it?*

JUDGE HARRY STONE
*NIGHT COURT*

doing new things becomes a matter of *morality*. Those pagans who "don't listen to God" and have the audacity to try new things are not only damned, they should be locked up.

For these dear souls, I have two quotes: "And the angel said unto them, 'Fear not: for, behold, I bring you good tidings of great joy, which shall be to all people'" (Luke 2:10). Those shepherds who were afraid to "try something new" (listening to an angel in a field) never made it to the manger. And then in 1 John 4:18: "There is no fear in love; but perfect love casteth out fear." This is my favorite method of expanding the comfort zone: Love it all.

In the air conditioning trade, "the comfort

zone" is the range of temperatures on the thermostat (usually around 72 degrees) in which neither heating nor air conditioning is needed. It's also called "the dead zone."

That's the result of honoring the comfort zone too much, too often: a sense of deadness; a feeling of being trapped in a life not of our desiring, doing things not of our choosing, spending time with people we don't like.

The answer? Do it.* Feel the fear, and do it anyway. *Physically move* to accomplish those things you choose. Eventually, learn to make friends with the Master Teacher fear.

Learn to love it all.

---

*This seems the ideal opportunity to recommend my book, *DO IT! Let's Get Off Our Buts.* At your local bookstore, or call 1-800-LIFE-101.

*Many a time*
*we've been down to*
*our last piece of fatback.*
*And I'd say,*
*"Should we eat it,*
*or render it down for soap?"*
*Your Uncle Jed would say,*
*"Render it down.*
*God will provide food*
*for us poor folks,*
*but we gotta*
*do our own washin'."*

GRANNY
*THE BEVERLY HILLBILLIES*

# Money

We have so many conflicting beliefs about money in our culture. Some are uplifting, some are "downpushing." It's little wonder that the way most people feel about money is simply *confused*.

If you want money, here's how to get it:

1. Reduce the number of limiting beliefs you have about money.
2. Increase the positive beliefs you hold.
3. Do what it takes to get money.

Money is simply a symbol o f energy. I use money so that, as an author, I don't have to carry books with me and trade them for whatever it is I want. ("How many scoops of vanilla fudge almond can I get for a book about life?")

It's a convenience. Can you imagine the chaos if you had to trade your marketable skills for the things you needed? Can you imagine a conversation between a secretary and the owner of a plum tree?

"I'd like some plums."

"What do you have to trade?"

"I can type a letter. I'll type a letter for a dozen plums."

"I don't have any letters."

"Well, then I'll type one for you."

"I don't need any letters. What else you got?"

"I can Xerox."

"I don't have any letters. I don't have anything to Xerox."

> *From birth to age 18,*
> *a girl needs good parents,*
> *from 18 to 35*
> *she needs good looks,*
> *from 35 to 55*
> *she needs a good personality,*
> *and from 55 on*
> *she needs cash.*
>
> SOPHIE TUCKER

"I can send a fax."

"Facts about what?"

"No, fax. Facsimile. You use it to send letters."

"How many times do I have to tell you? *I don't have any letters.*"

"What *do* you want?"

"I want a chicken."

"I don't have a chicken."

"Do you have a duck?"

"No."

"A goose?"

"I don't have any poultry of any kind."

"Do you have a color TV?"

"Yes."

"I'll trade you a dozen plums for a color TV."

"That's not a fair trade."

"All right. Two dozen plums. And a rooster."

"You have a rooster? I thought you wanted a chicken."

"The rooster wanted the chicken. I told him I'd help him out. But if I get a TV, I don't care about the rooster."

Do you see how much more cumbersome life would be if we had to barter for everything? Money, as a symbol of energy, makes it easier. For a certain amount of energy, you are given a symbol. You can then trade that symbol for something that requires someone else's energy.

Let's look at the limiting beliefs some people have about money. They aren't true, by the way. The one you want to *prove* to me is true is the very belief you would probably do best to *dis*prove for yourself—if you want more money, that is.

To disprove any of these, all you have to do is show that they are not true for *one person*. If one person did it, you can be number two. The statement, "All birds are red," can be disproved by finding just *one* bluebird.

**It takes money to make money.** There are stories galore of people who started with nothing—sometimes less than nothing (they inherited debts)—and made great fortunes. It takes effectiveness and perseverance, not money, to make money.

**Poor is pure.** Some of the grinding poverty I

> *Lack of money*
> *is the root of all evil.*
>
> GEORGE BERNARD SHAW

have seen is hardly "pure." It's often filthy, fly-ridden, and disease-laden. It doesn't seem to induce inner purity, either. Not that there aren't pure poor people. I, however, happen to think they'd be just as pure if they were rich. I have also met some people I'd consider pure who have lots of money.

**People resent rich people.** Some people resent rich people, some people resent poor people, some people resent people who resent other people. Some people also *respect* rich people.

**Wealthy people are snobby.** I've met some down-to-earth poor people, and I've met some dirt-poor snobs, too. Some people snub others for not being "enough"—not pretty enough, not smart enough, not evolved enough. Money's just one of the things snobby people get snobbish about, regardless of income level.

**It is easier for a camel to go through the eye of a needle than for a rich man to enter the Kingdom of God.** That's from the Bible, quoting Jesus (Matthew 19:24). Actually, it's not hard for a camel to get through the eye of the needle. I got through. "The needle" is the name of a gate in Jerusalem. The "eye" is the small doorway in the larger gate. When the main gate was closed, the eye would open. In order for a camel to pass through the eye of the needle, the camel must (a) stand in line (when the main gate is closed and only the eye is open, there tends to be a line); (b) have its cargo removed; and (c) go through on its knees (which camels have no trouble doing).

Knowing that Jesus often taught in parables, what do you suppose might have been the message? In order to enter the Kingdom of God (which Jesus said was "within" [Luke 17:21]), a rich man must (a) be patient; (b) unburden himself of his cargo (he can keep it, he just can't be attached to it); and (c) be humble, or in a symbolic posture of reverence (on his knees). That makes sense to me.

If you don't like this interpretation, there are stores for rich people that sell *great big* needles and *little teeny* stuffed camels. You can then sit all day long, if you so choose, putting a camel through the eye of a needle.

**Money is the root of all evil.** Back to the Bible. (Is it any wonder this has been called the world's

> If I were rich I'd have
> The time that I lack
> To sit in the
> Synagogue and pray,
> And maybe have a seat
> by the Eastern Wall.
>
> And I'd discuss the Holy Books
> With the learned men
> Seven hours every day.
> That would be the
> sweetest thing of all.
>
> SHELDON HARNICK
> FIDDLER ON THE ROOF

most misunderstood book?) This one's from 1 Timothy 6:10. The full sentence is, "The love of money is the root of all evil." In the New International translation, it reads, "The love of money is a root of *all kinds of* evil." In that sentence, a more accurate word for love is *lust*. The sentence then is, "Lusting after money is a root of all kinds of evil." I have no argument with that. Lusting after *anything* can be a root of all kinds of evil. Money in itself is neither good nor evil. It can be used for either, depending on the user's actions.

**You need training and education to get money.** There are many stories of people who made great fortunes, with which they endowed great educational institutions, while they themselves never graduated from elementary school. It's what you know and how you use it, not the amount of time you spent in school, that determines your ability to make money.

**Money can't buy me love.** As a friend of mine pointed out, "Whoever wrote that doesn't know where to shop."

**You can't take it with you.** True, but anywhere you can't take it, you wouldn't want it anyway.

**Money is too much responsibility.** If you have that much money, you can hire people to shoulder the burden of all that responsibility.

**It takes hard work to make money.** It takes *smart* work to make money. (In other words, being effective, not just efficient.)

**Money isn't everything.** No, but it's something.

**The best things in life are free.** As the same friend of mine pointed out, "Whoever wrote that doesn't shop where I shop."

**Money isn't spiritual or holy.** And poverty is? In fact, if you had lots of money, you could spend lots more time praying, meditating, buying yachts for your guru, putting a new wing on your church—whatever would help you get closer to God.

≈

Eliminating limiting beliefs about money is a good way to get more money. Another good way is enhancing *uplifting* beliefs. Just to show you I'm not

> **Lovey Howell:** *You know,*
> *I really wouldn't mind*
> *being poor, if it weren't*
> *for one thing.*
>
> **Thurston Howell III:**
> *What is that, my dear?*
>
> **Lovey:** *Poverty.*

the only one who has a high regard for money, here's what some other people have said in praise of money:

- Money is a sweet balm. *(Arabian proverb)*

- Money is a guarantee that we may have what we want in the future. Though we need nothing at the moment, it insures the possibility of satisfying a necessary desire when it arises. *(Aristotle)*

- Money is the sovereign queen of all

delights—for her, the lawyer pleads, the soldier fights. *(Richard Barnfield)*

- Money is the symbol of everything that is necessary for man's well-being and happiness. Money means freedom, independence, liberty. *(Edward E. Beals)*

- Money is the sinews of art and literature. *(Samuel Butler)*

- Money is Aladdin's lamp. *(Lord Byron)*

- Money is the representative of a certain quantity of corn or other commodity. Its value is in the necessities of the animal man. It is so much warmth, so much bread. *(Ralph Waldo Emerson)*

- Money is like an arm or a leg—use it or lose it. *(Henry Ford)*

- Money is health, and liberty, and strength. *(Charles Lamb)*

- Money is the sixth sense which enables you to enjoy the other five. *(Somerset Maugham)*

- Money is that which brings honor, friends, conquest, and realms. *(John Milton)*

- Money is the only substance which can keep a cold world from nicknaming a

> *A private railroad car*
> *is not an acquired taste.*
> *One takes to it immediately.*
>
> ELEANOR R. BELMONT

citizen "Hey, you!" *(Wilson Mizner)*

- Money is the cause of good things to a good man, of evil things to a bad man. *(Philo)*

- Money is human happiness in the abstract. *(Arthur Schopenhauer)*

- Money is the most important thing in the world. *(George Bernard Shaw)*

- Money is an article which may be used as a universal passport to everywhere except heaven, and as a universal provider for everything except happiness. *(Wall Street Journal)*

- Money is the root of all good. *(Rudolf Wanderone)*

Here are some suggestions on how to have more money:

1. Remember that money is just a *symbol* of *energy*. What you do with the energy will determine the money's effect on you and those around you.

2. Money is a method—not an intention, belief, or experience. Money in and of itself will not make you happy, joyful, fulfilled, content, or anything else. It will make you *rich*, but that, too, is a symbol. Money is a tool. You can build things with tools, but the tool is not the thing you want built.

3. Be open to receiving money from any source, in any amount, in any form, at any time. Learn to say, "Yes, thank you," when people offer you things that have financial value.

4. Be open to spend. Life is cycles of giving and receiving. We breathe in, we breathe out. The exhale is as important as the inhale. If we stop inhaling or exhaling for any period of time, life becomes remarkably uncomfortable. Also, keeping the money flowing about you allows for more of the *experiences* you wanted the money for in the first place.

5. Affirm money. Use affirmations that contain

> *Money-giving is*
> *a very good criterion*
> *of a person's mental health.*
> *Generous people are*
> *rarely mentally ill people.*
>
> DR. KARL A. MENNINGER

the words, *money, cash, dollars,* and so on. (As with the word *death,* we seem to avoid using the word *money.* If you want money, ask for money.) "I am enjoying the large sums of money that flow into my life, quickly and effortlessly, this or something better for the highest good of all concerned."

6. Give 10% away. This is called tithing. By giving 10% away (to your church, your favorite charity, any cause *you* believe in), you are not only passing some energy along for good use, you are saying, "Thank you. I have more than I need." This is a major statement of abundance. Be a joyful giver so that you can

also be a joyful receiver.

7. Enjoy the money you have. If you think you don't have enough to enjoy yourself now, you will probably not have enough when you have millions. Remove the "unfun" you may have attached to money. Take some money and do something *enjoyable*. Right now.

8. Be grateful for the money you already have. When I was in Egypt, I stopped at a town on the banks of the Nile. The richest man in town had something no one else in town had. It was this one possession that made him the richest man in town. Everyone knew he was the richest man in town because he had this. With great pride he showed it to me. What do you think it was? A TV? A dishwasher? A blender? No. The town had no electricity. A bathtub? A sink? A toilet? No. The town had no running water. The man was the richest man in town because he had a *cement floor*. It was cracked, it was filthy, it was falling apart, but he was proud of it because everyone else's floor was dirt. Be grateful for the money (and things you bought with the money) you have.

9. I don't have a number 9, but most lists of ten things have a number 9, so I thought this one might as well.

10. Keep 10% of your increase as a "money magnet." Keep it, in cash or tangible valuables. As it grows, it attracts money to you. How? The more you have, the less anxiety you feel

> *Money is better than poverty,*
> *if only for financial reasons.*
>
> WOODY ALLEN

about money; therefore the more you are likely to get.

*I don't like money, actually,*
*but it quiets my nerves.*

JOE LOUIS

*A friend is a gift
you give yourself.*

ROBERT LOUIS STEVENSON

# The Power of Partnership

The support you can gather from good friends, groups, and your Master Teacher is formidable. The encouragement you can give them in return (yes, even Master Teachers need a little encouragement) is substantial.

To use your goals and aspirations as small talk over dinner dissipates their energy. But to meet with like minds and discuss the challenges and triumphs of mastering your life; *that* has power, splendor, and esteem.

- Friends are, of course, invaluable—for both creation and recreation. People who love us for what we are, not what we have already done, are great support when we're trying to do and be more.

- You can form or join a support group of like-minded people moving in a similar direction. Regular meetings at which victories are celebrated, problems solved, and new ideas brainstormed, can be one of the best ways to produce ongoing results.

- Professional counselors, advisors, and consultants are available—at a price, of course—but the insight and wisdom they can impart in a brief session may be priceless.

- Books, tapes, lectures, and courses of all kinds make you "partners" with the finest minds of

*Nothing shortens a journey so pleasantly*
*as an account of misfortunes*
*at which the hearer*
*is permitted to laugh.*

QUENTIN CRISP

all time. Just because people aren't there "in person" doesn't mean there's not a relationship between you and them. For the most part, people take the time to write a book, make a tape, or teach a course because they *care*. Be the beneficiary of their knowledge, experience, and caring.

- Lest I forget, you have many Master Teachers—and your own personal Master Teacher, who is always with you. Spend time in your sanctuary with your Master Teacher. Learn to listen to your Master Teacher's voice throughout the day. Let the dialogue between the two of you be ongoing.

*One looks back with appreciation*
*to the brilliant teachers,*
*but with gratitude to those*
*who touched our human feelings.*
*The curriculum is so much*
*necessary raw material,*
*but warmth is the vital element*
*for the growing plant*
*and for the soul of the child.*

CARL JUNG

*I think and think*
*for months and years.*
*Ninety-nine times,*
*the conclusion is false.*
*The hundredth time*
*I am right.*

ALBERT EINSTEIN

# How Much Is Enough?

People often wonder: How long will this take? How much work is enough? How much affirming, planning, and acting must I do to get what I want?

The answer is very simple: when you have what you want, it was enough.

This is not the answer most people want to hear. We are so used to delivery schedules and travel timetables that precisely pinpoint when it (or we) will arrive, it's often hard to accept the ancient wisdom, "It'll shine when it shines."

Sorry. That is the only answer I have.

Our estimates of time are only estimates—best guesses. Some things will happen sooner, some later. If your goal is not reached in the time frame you set, set a new time frame. Do whatever else needs to be done to succeed. When you've done all that and it's still not enough, do some more. When do you stop doing? When you've gotten what you want.

People sometimes stop when they are *so close* to their goals because they become discouraged. When you take the *dis* off *discourage,* you have what you need to press on: courage.

Do whatever it takes to achieve what you want. Don't accept the limitations of other people who claim things are "unchangeable." If it's written in stone, bring your hammer and chisel.

When you have what you want, that was enough.

*I am open to receive*
*With every breath I breathe.*

MICHAEL SUN

# Receiving

Some people select their goals, do the necessary work, and *still* don't have what they want. These people need to do more work—but maybe it's not *external* work. Maybe it's on themselves.

When we work for something, we must be open to receive. This may seem silly, but some people have some rather definite limits on *what* they can receive and *how* they can receive it. If you try to give them a million dollars, they'll accept it, but *only if* the million dollars is in new $100 bills and delivered to the back door, at 4:15 sharp, next Wednesday.

If we want more, it's helpful to know how to *receive* more. We receive more by saying, "Yes." If they want to give you a million dollars in pennies, take it. If they want you to pick them up, say you'll be right over. If they want to deliver the money, tell 'em, "Pick your door."

Just as you have many methods and behaviors for fulfilling your desires and intentions, life has many ways to give you what you've been asking for.

Remember, too, that you are worthy of all the good that comes your way. How do I know? If you weren't worthy, it wouldn't come your way. If you want a relationship, and someone "over and above" your dreams appears on your doorstep with flowers and candy, don't say, "You must have the wrong house"—*invite the lucky person in.*

*Gladness of the heart
is the life of a man,
and the joyfulness of a man
prolongeth his days.*

ECCLESIASTICUS

30:22

# PART FIVE

## TO HAVE JOY AND TO HAVE IT MORE ABUNDANTLY

There is no end to joy—no upper limit. When you think you've had all the joy you can tolerate, you've only reached *your* limit, not joy's. Use that moment to expand your limit.

Don't just increase joy by a little. Double it. Then, double that. Discover that your capacity to know joy is as limitless as joy itself.

As limitless as you.

> *The human race,*
> *to which so many*
> *of my readers belong,*
> *has been playing*
> *at children's games*
> *from the beginning,*
> *which is a nuisance*
> *for the few people who grow up.*

G. K. CHESTERTON

1904

# Grow Up!

Ever watch someone have a temper tantrum? Or go on and on about how unfairly the world treated her? Or cry over the loss of a love he didn't much like anyway? Ever watch a fit of jealousy, pettiness, or vindictiveness?

On those occasions, didn't you want to quote Joan Rivers: *"Grow up!"*

I'm not talking about child*like* qualities—joy, playfulness, spontaneity. I'm talking about child*ish* traits—spoiled, infantile, inconsiderate.

This sort of immaturity hurts and offends not just those around us; it hurts and offends *us*. Even while we're doing it, we know, "This isn't right." Even through the anger, fear, and separation, we know, "This isn't necessary."

And it's not. It's time to mature, to ripen, to grow up.

*I don't have*
*a warm personal enemy left.*
*They've all died off.*
*I miss them terribly*
*because*
*they helped define me.*

Claire Booth Luce

# Heal the Past

What hurts about the past is our *memory*. We remember the pain of an event, and we hurt again. Fortunately, we can heal the memories of the past.

One technique is to go into your sanctuary (remembering to let the light at your entryway surround, fill, protect, bless, and heal you for your highest good), sit in front of the video screen, and, on the screen, watch the memory that is causing the pain. The "halo" around the screen is dark. Let the memory play itself out. (If the images are difficult, you might ask your Master Teacher to join you. Master Teachers are great for holding hands, giving comfort, and instilling courage.)

Then let the image fade. Let the white light around the screen glow brightly. Then see the same scene *the way you wanted it to be*. What do you wish had happened? See it. What do you wish you had said? Hear yourself saying it. How do you wish others had responded? See them responding that way. What would you like to have felt? Feel that.

Replacing a negative memory with a positive one heals it.

You can also use your health center. Perhaps there is a special memory-healing device or magic elixir or a master with a touch that heals. Whatever you wish medical science had that would heal the past, imagine it in your health center, and use it.

If the hurt involves other people, you can invite them into your sanctuary. Under the guidance and

*Events in the past*
*may be roughly divided*
*into those which probably never happened*
*and those which do not matter.*

W. R. INGE

DEAN OF ST. PAUL'S, LONDON

protection of your Master Teacher, you can tell them whatever it is you want them to know, forgive them (and yourself), and let them go into that pure, white light of the people mover.

There's no need to dwell on the past, remembering every little painful detail and then healing it. Just heal what surfaces on its own, and move on with your life—your present.

*Memory, the priestess,*
*kills the present*
*and offers its heart*
*on the shrine of the dead past.*

RABINDRANATH TAGORE

*Of one thing I am certain,*
*the body is not*
*the measure of healing*
*—peace is the measure.*

George Melton

*Health is the state about which*
*medicine has nothing to say.*

W. H. Auden

# Health

Health is more than just the lack of illness—health is aliveness, energy, joy.

By always focusing on eliminating illness, few of us learn how to enhance health—or even that enhancing health is possible. It is.

You don't have to be sick to get better.

Health is not just for the body. Health includes the mind, the emotions, the whole person. Health is the amount of vibrant, peaceful, loving energy flowing through your being. The more energy, the greater the health.

Let that energy flow in you, through you.

Health is not heavy. Health is light work.

*God may forgive you,*
*but I never can.*

Elizabeth I

1533–1603

# For Giving

Forgiving means "for giving"—*in favor of* giving.

When you forgive another, to whom do you give? The other? Sometimes. Yourself? Always. To forgive another is being in favor of giving to yourself.

In addition, most of us judge ourselves more harshly and more often than we judge others. It's important to forgive ourselves for all the things we hold against ourselves.

There is a third judgment to forgive: the fact that we judged in the first place. When we judge, we leave our happiness behind—sometimes *way* behind. We know this, and we judge ourselves for having judged.

The layers of forgiveness, then, are: first, the person we judged (ourselves or another); and, second, ourselves for having judged in the first place.

The technique? Simple.

Say to yourself, "I forgive _____ (NAME OF THE PERSON, PLACE, OR THING YOU JUDGED, INCLUDING YOURSELF) f o r _____ (THE 'TRANSGRESSION'). I forgive myself for judging _____ (SAME PERSON, PLACE, OR THING, INCLUDING YOURSELF) for _____ (WHAT YOU JUDGED)."

That's it. Simple, but amazingly effective. You can say it out loud, or say it to yourself.

If you have a lot to forgive one person for, you might want to invite that person into your sanctu-

> *Of course God will forgive me;*
> *that's his business.*

HEINRICH HEINE

LAST WORDS

1856

ary and forgive the person there. (Ask your Master Teacher to come along, if you like.)

That's all there is to forgiveness. Simple but powerful. How powerful? Try it for five minutes. See what happens.

*The American public*
*would forgive me anything*
*except running off*
*with Eddie Fisher.*


JACQUELINE KENNEDY

1964

*Education is*
*what survives when*
*what has been learned*
*has been forgotten.*

B. F. SKINNER

# For Getting

After you've forgiven the transgression and judgment, there's only one thing to do: forget them. Whatever "protection" you think you may gain from remembering all your past grievances is far less important than the balm of forgetting.

What's the value in forgetting? It's all in the word: for getting—to be in favor of getting, of receiving.

We sometimes think that shaking a fist (threateningly, with all the remembered transgressions) is the way to get something. A shaking fist tends to beget a shaking (or swinging) fist.

To receive, for give. To get, for get.

Remembering a grievance locks you into remembering hurt, pain, anger, betrayal, and disappointment. Who on earth wants *that?* Let it go. *For give* it away. Then *for get* something new and better (light-er) in its place.

Heal the memories. Forgive the past. Then forget it. Let it go. It is not worth remembering. None of it's worth remembering. What's worth *experiencing* is the joy of this moment.

To get it, for get.

*The children despise
their parents until the age of forty,
when they suddenly
become just like them
—thus preserving the system.*

QUENTIN CREWE

# Parents

Why, just when we were feeling all joyful, did I have to bring *them* up? Well, they brought *us* up, so, for a moment, allow me to bring *them* up.

It may seem that I have been harsh on parents in this book. When explaining why we feel unworthy, think negatively, or aren't happy, I often returned to the childhood, and there loomed Mom and Dad.

Yes, I am guilty of that, and I now make my amends with these thoughts:

**1. Your childhood is over.** *You* are now in charge of your life. You can't blame the past—or anyone in it—for what you do *today*. Even if you can formulate a convincing argument to the contrary, it does you no good. Your childhood is gone. It's past.

Blaming the past is like blaming gravity for the glass you broke. Yes, without gravity, the glass would not have fallen. But you *know* about gravity and you *know* about glasses and you *know* what happens when you combine gravity, a falling glass, and a hard surface.

Your childhood is like gravity. It was what it was. Your life today is like the glass. Handle it with care. If it breaks, clean up the mess, and get another glass (your life tomorrow) from the cupboard.

**2. Your parents did the best they could with what they knew.** Like you, your parents weren't given an instruction manual for life. They had to learn it as they went along. They had to learn how

> *My mother had*
> *a great deal of trouble with me,*
> *but I think she enjoyed it.*
>
> MARK TWAIN

to make a living, run a home, get along with each other, and raise a baby (you) all at the same time. No easy task. Along the way, they made lots of mistakes. They weren't the perfect parents. But, let's face it, you weren't the perfect child, either.

**3. How you turned out is mostly a result of genetics anyway.**

**4. Your parents gave you the greatest gift of all: Life.** Whatever else they did or didn't do, if not for them, you wouldn't be here. They deserve a big thank-you for that.

You don't have to *like* your parents. But it feels better if you learn to love them.

*If you really want to hear about it,*
*the first thing you'll probably*
*want to know is where I was born,*
*and what my lousy childhood was likc,*
*and how my parents were occupied*
*and all before they had me,*
*and all that David Copperfield*
*kind of crap, but I don't feel like*
*going into it.*

J. D. Salinger
*Catcher in the Rye*

*Laughter is*
*inner jogging.*

NORMAN COUSINS

# Laughter

Laugh. Out loud. Often.

Laughter's good for you—which may be too bad. If it raised the cholesterol count or had too many calories, people might do it more often. If laughter were only *forbidden*, then people would do it all the time. We'd have laugh police. If they caught you laughing, they'd write you a ticket. Children's TV programming would have to be monitored very carefully. We wouldn't want anyone pushing humor on innocent young minds. "What are you kids doing in there?" "We're drinking beer and smoking cigarettes." "Okay, but no laughing."

**Pop Quiz! Which is funniest:**

(A) "I was gratified to be able to answer promptly. I said I don't know." (Mark Twain)

(B) "Aristotle was famous for knowing everything. He taught that the brain exists merely to cool the blood and is not involved in the process of thinking. This is true only of certain persons." (Will Cuppy)

(C) "The school of hard knocks is an accelerated curriculum." (Menander)

(D) "I knew I was an unwanted baby when I saw that my bath toys were a toaster and a radio." (Joan Rivers)

(E) "My parents put a live Teddy bear in my crib." (Woody Allen)

(F) "Never lend your car to anyone to whom you have given birth." (Erma Bombeck)

(G) Life is like laughing with a cracked rib.

*Tears, idle tears,*
*I know not what they mean,*
*Tears from the depth*
*of some divine despair*
*Rise in the heart,*
*and gather to the eyes,*
*In looking on the happy*
*autumn fields,*
*And thinking of the days*
*that are no more.*

ALFRED, LORD TENNYSON

1847

# Tears

Crying, like laughing, is a marvelous, natural release. People feel *so good* after a cry, I wonder why it's such a taboo.

People come pouring out of a movie theater, sniffling and dripping—you'd think they'd set off a tear gas canister. You ask them, "What happened?" fully expecting the story of a disaster. They sob, "That was the best movie I ever saw." (One wants to remind them that the correct grammar necessitates, "That was the best movie I *have* ever *seen*," but they seem so upset already.)

Tears are natural to healing *and* enjoying. Intense feelings of gratitude, awe, and compassion are often accompanied by tears. "Moved to tears," as they say.

Allow yourself to be moved by your life, not just the movies.

*To live content with small means;*
*to seek elegance rather than luxury,*
*and refinement rather than fashion;*
*to be worthy, not respectable,*
*and wealthy, not rich;*
*to study hard, think quietly,*
*talk gently, act frankly;*
*to listen to stars and birds,*
*to babes and sages,*
*with open heart;*
*to bear all cheerfully,*
*do all bravely,*
*await occasions, hurry never.*
*In a word, to let the spiritual,*
*unbidden and unconscious,*
*grow up through the common.*
*This is to be my symphony.*

WILLIAM HENRY CHANNING

1810–1884

# Wealth

Unlike money, wealth is not just what you have. Wealth is what you can do without.

Who is wealthier, the person who is addicted to something and has plenty of money to buy it, or the person who doesn't desire the addictive substance at all?

Wealthy people carry their riches within. The less they need of this physical world, the wealthier they are. They may or may not have large sums of money. It matters not. Whatever they have is fine.

Wealth is health, happiness, abundance, prosperity, riches, loving, caring, sharing, learning, knowing what we want, opportunity, enjoying, and balance.

Wealth is enjoying one's own company.

Wealth is being able to love oneself fully.*

*This seems the ideal opportunity to recommend my book *WEALTH 101: Wealth Is Much More Than Money.* At your local bookstore, or call 1-800-LIFE-101.

*Don't go to piano bars*
*where young,*
*unemployed actors*
*get up and sing.*
*Definitely don't <u>be</u> a young,*
*unemployed actor who*
*gets up and sings.*

TONY LANG

# Sacrifice

You would be far happier if you gave up certain things. This may not be easy for you. I nonetheless suggest you give them up—go cold turkey—starting right now, this minute, before you turn the page.

*Give* is a nice word. *Up* is a nice word. Put them together, and people can get awfully nasty. "I'm not going to give up *anything*. And *sacrifice*. That's even *worse* than giving up. Sacrifice means giving up something *really* good."

Maybe not. I think you'd be better off sacrificing greed, lust, hurt, judgments, demands, spoiledness, envy, jealousy, vindictiveness.

Did you think I was going to ask you to give up *good* stuff? Most people think that sacrifice means giving up *only* the good stuff. Not so. The negative stuff, the cold stuff, the hard stuff—you can sacrifice those, too.

And you can give them *up*. Surrender them to the higher part of yourself. Surround them with light. Let them go.

You don't need them anymore.

*The Sea of Galilee*
*and the Dead Sea*
*are made of the same water.*
*It flows down, clear and cool,*
*from the heights of Hermon*
*and the roots of the cedars of Lebanon.*
*The Sea of Galilee makes beauty of it,*
*for the Sea of Galilee has an outlet.*
*It gets to give.*
*It gathers in its riches that*
*it may pour them out again*
*to fertilize the Jordan plain.*
*But the Dead Sea*
*with the same water makes horror.*
*For the Dead Sea has no outlet.*
*It gets to keep.*

HARRY EMERSON FOSDICK
*THE MEANING OF SERVICE*

1920

# Service

The idea that life is take, take, take (learn, learn, learn) needs to be balanced with the idea that life is also giving (teaching). Receiving and giving (learning and teaching) are two parts of a single flow, like breathing in (receiving) and breathing out (giving). One cannot take place without the other.

We inhale oxygen and exhale carbon dioxide. Plants absorb the carbon dioxide and release oxygen. The cycle is complete. This connection between giving and receiving is fundamental to life.

What is waste to animals is essential to plants, and vice versa. Our own taking from and giving to life is just as intimately connected.

We seem to be students of those who know more than we do, doers with those who know just about as much as we do, and teachers of those who know less than we do. Life is a process of doing, learning, enjoying, *and* teaching.

In ten minutes on the job, you might learn how to transfer a call on the new phone system, consult with a co-worker on a method for increasing sales, and teach someone how to load paper into the copy machine. And this learning-doing-teaching can take place with the same person.

This learning-doing-teaching happens in almost every area of life—and all three often happen simultaneously. The child we are teaching to read and write is, in the same moment, teaching us innocence and wonder.

> **Boy:** *Teach me*
> *what you know, Jim.*
>
> **Reverend Jim:** *That would*
> *take hours, Terry.*
> *Ah, what the heck!*
> *We've all got a little*
> *Obi Wan Kenobie in us.*
>
> TAXI

When we give a stranger directions, why do we feel so good? Because giving is a natural part of life. If we're lost and somebody puts us on the right track, that feels good, too. Receiving is also a natural part of life.

When we learn to give to ourselves so fully that our cup overflows, then we may be called to be of service.

Service is not a chore. Service is a privilege.

In truth, giving is not just a natural act; it hurts *not* to give. We see the pain in another, and we want to ease the hurt. We see someone lost, and want to help them find the way.

Sometimes our gift is a hug or a kind word or

the right bit of information at the right moment. Perhaps it's a smile or a sigh or a laugh. And maybe you cry with someone—or for them.

There is no need to seek students, just as there is no need to seek lessons. When the teacher is ready, the student appears.

When the server is ready, the service appears.

*Tomorrow is the most
important thing in life.
Comes into us at midnight
very clean.
It's perfect when it arrives
and it puts itself
in our hands.
It hopes we've
learned something
from yesterday.*

JOHN WAYNE

# The Attitude of Gratitude

The word *gratitude* comes from the root *gratus*, which means pleasing. The obvious interpretation is that when you are pleased with something, you are grateful. A second interpretation—the more radical, and therefore the one I prefer—is that when you are grateful, *then* you are pleased, not by the thing, but by the gratitude.

In other words, to feel pleased, be grateful.

We have so much to be grateful for. Alas, it's part of human behavior to take good things for granted. It's biological, actually. A part of our brain filters out whatever isn't hurtful, fearful, or physically moving. This filtering helped our forebears separate the beasts from the rocks and the trees.

Today, this same device starts filtering out all the good things we have, almost as soon as we get them. After a week or month or year with something that initially was *wonderful*, we have grown accustomed to it. We take it for granted.

What to do? Counteract complacency. *Consciously* be grateful for the good in your life. Make lists. Have gratitude flings. Be thankful for little things, big things, every thing.

Appreciate the things that are so magnificent, you took them for granted decades ago. What am I talking about? Your senses. Quick! Name all five! Some people can name the five Great Lakes faster than name their own senses. Let's not forget the brain and the body and the emotions, and walking,

> *Let us be thankful for the fools.*
> *But for them*
> *the rest of us could not succeed.*
>
> MARK TWAIN

talking, thumbs. Thumbs? Sure: Try to pick up some things without using your thumbs.

As Dale Evans once said, "I'm so busy loving *everybody*, I don't have any time to hate *anybody.*" When you start noticing even a small portion of all there is to be grateful for, you'll find there's no room for lack, hurt, or want.

The attitude of gratitude: the great, full feeling.

*Rest and be thankful.*

Inscription on a Stone Seat
in the Scottish Highlands

*Happiness is having
a large, loving, caring,
close-knit family
in another city.*

GEORGE BURNS

# It Takes Strength to Be Happy

Happiness is not easy. It's not for the weak, the timid, the wishy-washy, the easily dissuaded, or the uncertain.

Happiness is not for wimps.

Happiness requires courage, stamina, persistence, fortitude, perseverance, bravery, boldness, valor, vigor, concentration, solidity, substance, backbone, grit, guts, moxie, nerve, pluck, resilience, spunk, tenacity, tolerance, will power, chutzpah, and a good thesaurus.

If you think happiness is easy, think again. The *theory* of happiness is simple; so simple, in fact, it can be stated in a parenthesis ("to be happy, think happy thoughts") in the middle of a not-very-long sentence. The successful *implementation* of that theory—that's where the courage, stamina, etc., come in.

Our lives are full of happy things we can think happy thoughts about. If we run out of those, there are books, music, and movies full of happy thoughts. All we have to do is focus on the happy things to think happy thoughts, which will make us happy. That's all.

THEN WHY THE HELL AREN'T WE HAPPY ALL THE TIME!!??

With the pressures and distractions we've already discussed—the Fight or Flight Response, the

> *We confide in our strength,*
> *without boasting of it;*
> *we respect that of others,*
> *without fearing it.*
>
> THOMAS JEFFERSON

inaccurate yet all-pervading feeling of unworthiness, habits, addictions, brain parts that filter out good stuff, heredity, and so on—is it any wonder that thinking happy thoughts takes some *strength*.

It also takes practice, patience, and discipline. It's not an easy challenge, but when you're through, you'll know you've done your work and done it well. You'll be among the strong, the proud, the few.

Be all that you can be. Join the happy.

*Do you really think it is weakness
that yields to temptation?
I tell you that there are terrible
temptations which it requires strength,
strength and courage,
to yield to.*

OSCAR WILDE

*If you don't like
what you're doing,
you can always
pick up your needle and
move to another groove.*

TIMOTHY LEARY

# You Don't *Have* to Do Anything

Really. You don't. Well, yes, a few biological things, but for the most part, everything you do you do because you're *choosing* to do it. You might as well admit that. At least to yourself. It makes life easier.

"Have to" implies need, and need is food-shelter-clothing. Everything else is just a "want." Therefore, unless it's doing something to put a scrap of food in your mouth, a few rags on your back, or a temporary roof over your head, you don't *have to* do it.

All those things you think you *have* to do, you can tell yourself, "I don't have to _____," and fill in the blank. It's quite liberating. It feels good. Then if you *choose* to do whatever you declared you don't *have* to do, that's fine.

You can add, "And what I choose to do, I can do." Because you can.

*Learn the art of patience.*
*Apply discipline to your thoughts*
*when they become anxious*
*over the outcome of a goal.*
*Impatience breeds anxiety,*
*fear, discouragement*
*and failure.*
*Patience creates*
*confidence, decisiveness*
*and a rational outlook,*
*which eventually leads to success.*

BRIAN ADAMS

# Hurry Up and Be Patient!

The sooner you're patient, the easier your life will become. Really. When you're patient, you can relax and enjoy the ride. Life has its own timing. Although perfect, life often disagrees with our timetables.

You feel *so good* about life when you're patient. I would suggest that you not delay a moment. Obtain patience at your earliest opportunity. It makes obtaining everything else much easier, and much more fun. And if you *don't* get *all* of what you want, that's okay, because you're patient.

Some people like to doctor life—they think they can "fix" it. Life doesn't need a doctor. It's not sick. As KungFucious said, "If you want to doctor life, maybe you need to be patient."

Speaking of doctors, have I told you of all the health problems that can be caused by impatience? Do you know how much stress getting sick causes the body? A lot. People get sick from it. It's best to avoid all that. Your life may depend on how quickly you can get patient.

Not that I want to rush you. Do it in your own time. But hurry.

I just hate to see anyone suffer needlessly. You can start by taking a deep breath—all the way down into your lower abdomen. Hurry up and do it before you have to do something else, so you can take your time. That's important.

There. Doesn't that feel better? That's the be-

> *He ranged his tropes,*
> *and preached up patience;*
> *Backed his opinion*
> *with quotations.*
>
> MATTHEW PRIOR
>
> 1708

ginning of patience.

Well, I don't want to write more than two pages on patience, and I'm running out of room. I hope I have impressed on you the dire need to be patient. But there's no hurry. If you're impatient, be patient with that. Unless, of course, you have trouble enjoying the moment, in which case, rather than being patient with impatience, you might as well be patient with life, and I'm running out of room for this chapter so I have to run now. By the way, the key to patience is acceptance.

*I'm extraordinarily patient provided
I get my own way in the end.*

MARGARET THATCHER

*We are here and it is now.*
*Further than that,*
*all knowledge is moonshine.*

H. L. Mencken

# Live Now

What a strange title for a chapter. "Live Now." When *else* are we supposed to live? Now, of course. But many people spend a lot of time (that precious commodity for getting what you want) in the past—remembering things that happened, and getting upset about them.

Other people spend a lot of time in the future, worrying about this, that, and something else—most of which probably will never come to pass. (F.E.A.R. = False Expectations Appearing Real.)

Some people are bi-timers. They can say "bye" to the present and go zipping off into the past *and* the future simultaneously.

What happened to the moment? No, don't answer that. You have to go back in the past to do so. What about *this* moment. Oops. Gone. It's easier to pick up quicksilver than to capture the moment.

So don't capture it. There's nothing to capture. It's all here—present, although perhaps slightly unaccounted for. There's nothing to struggle with. When you come back from the past or the future, the present will always be here, waiting.

It won't be the *same* present, of course. As Heraclitus observed around 500 B.C. (talk about the past), "You cannot step twice into the same river; for other waters are always flowing on to you." Thus it is with time.

The irony is that there's nowhere to go. It's all here, now, in the moment. The further irony is that

> *Getting there isn't half the fun—*
> *it's all the fun.*
>
> ROBERT TOWNSEND

you *can't* go anywhere, even if you tried. If you're in the "past" or the "future," you're not in those places at all. You're *thinking* and *feeling* about them —but you're thinking and feeling about the past and future *right now.* In the present.

We are *always* in the present, no matter what we do, no matter where we "go." If someone insists, "Come present!" tell them, "I was present—with my thoughts. If you do something more interesting than my thoughts, I'll pay attention to you." *That* should bring them present.

"Live Now." What a strange title for a chapter.

*I still lived in the future—*
*a habit which is the death of happiness.*

QUENTIN CRISP

*She knows what is the*
*best purpose of education:*
*not to be frightened*
*by the best*
*but to treat it*
*as part of daily life.*

JOHN MASON BROWN

# Worthiness

There is nothing you need to do to become worthy. You already *are* worthy. You don't even have to discover your worthiness. You can feel utterly worthless and still be worthy.

People have said, "I don't feel worthy to be alive." But you *are* alive; therefore you *must* be worthy. It's very simple: if you're not worth life, you don't have it.

Worthiness is a given. It has nothing to do with action, thoughts, feelings, mind, body, emotions, or anything else. You are worthy of being because you *are.* Period. End of chapter.

*So much is a man worth
as he esteems himself.*

FRANÇOIS RABELAIS

1532

# Worthiness, Part Two

"If I'm worthy just because I am, how come I don't *feel* worthy?"

You're not talking about worthiness. You're talking about *self-esteem*. If you want to think better about yourself and feel better about yourself, learn to improve your self-esteem.

"How do I improve self-esteem?"

Next chapter.

*Ofttimes nothing
profits more
Than self-esteem,
grounded on
just and right
Well managed.*

JOHN MILTON

1667

# Self-Esteem

Self-esteem is how you think and feel about yourself—how you *regard* yourself.

If you were taught that you *must* be perfect, then your self-esteem might be pretty low—humans are notoriously not perfect. Or, maybe you were taught that everything you do and whatever you do is perfect, in which case, your self-esteem might be pretty high.

Increasing your self-esteem is easy. You simply do good things, *and remember that you did them.*

Most people already *do* enough good for some high-level self-esteem. Alas, people tend to *forget*. They do so much good, most of it's taken for granted and forgotten as soon as it's done.

Make a list of all the good you do. Then review the list. Often. Take note of the often-overlooked good you do. Did you bathe in the past forty-eight hours? Very good. Brush your teeth, too? Terrific. Use deodorant? Excellent. You've done your part in the fight against indoor air pollution. Put those on your list.

Take note of your moment-by-moment life: the people you smile at, the pedestrians you stop for, the friends you support, the relatives you're nice to, the boss (or employees) you put up with. The list goes on and on.

Honestly—you're a pretty decent human being, aren't you? Of course you are. How do I know? Nasty, wicked people don't read books such as this.

> *Men stumble over the truth*
> *from time to time,*
> *but most pick themselves up*
> *and hurry off*
> *as if nothing happened.*
>
> SIR WINSTON CHURCHILL

If they do, they certainly don't get as far as page 442.

You're great—warm, witty, friendly, kind, compassionate. Now if you only had a better memory so you could remember all this without having to buy books to remind you, you'd be perfect.

*If the grass is greener*
*in the other fellow's yard,*
*let him worry about cutting it.*

FRED ALLEN

*Sometimes*
*I sits and thinks,*
*and sometimes*
*I just sits.*

SATCHEL PAIGE

# Meditate, Contemplate, or "Just Sits"

In addition to visualization, you might like to try any number of meditative and contemplative techniques available—or you might just want to sit quietly and relax.

Whenever you meditate, contemplate, pray, do spiritual exercises, or "just sits," it's good to ask the white light to surround, fill, and protect you, knowing only that which is for your highest good and the highest good of all concerned will take place during your quiet time. You may want to do your meditation in your sanctuary.

Before starting, prepare your physical environment. Arrange not to be disturbed. Unplug the phone. Put a note on the door. Wear ear plugs if noises might distract you. (I like the soft foam-rubber kind sold under such trade names as E.A.R., HUSHER, and DECIDAMP.) Take care of your bodily needs. Have some water nearby if you get thirsty, and maybe some tissues, too.

**Contemplation** is thinking *about* something, often something uplifting. You could contemplate any of the hundreds of quotes or ideas in this book. Often, when we hear a new and potentially useful idea, we say, "I'll have to think about that." Contemplation is a good time to "think about that," to consider the truth of it, to imagine the changes and improvements it might make in your life.

Or, you could contemplate a nonverbal object,

> *What would you*
> *attempt to do*
> *if you knew*
> *you could not fail?*
>
> DR. ROBERT SCHULLER

such as a flower, or a concept, such as God. The idea of contemplation is to set aside a certain amount of quiet time to think about just *that*, whatever you decide "that" will be.

**Meditation.** There are so many techniques of meditation, taught by so many books and organizations, that it's hard to define the word properly.

You might want to try various meditations to see what they're like. With meditation, please keep in mind that *you'll never know until you do it*. We may like to think we know what the effects of a given meditation will be by just reading the description, but I suggest you try it and *then* decide.

**Breathing Meditation.** Sit comfortably, close

your eyes, and simply be aware of your breath. Follow it in and out. Don't "try" to breathe; don't consciously alter your rhythm of breathing; just follow the breath as it naturally flows in and out. If you get lost in thoughts, return to your breath.

**Mantras.** Some people like to add a word or sound to help the mind focus as the breath goes in and out. Some people use *one* or *God* or *AUM (OHM)* or *love*. These—or any others—are fine. As you breathe in, say to yourself, mentally, "love." As you breathe out, "love." If you don't like synchronizing sounds to breath, don't. It doesn't matter.

It's not so much the *sound,* but the *meaning you assign* to the sound. You may use a mantra such as "Ummmm" just because it sounds good—satisfying and relaxing. Or you may say "Ahhhh" represents the pure sound of God. Because you *say* it does, it will.

**Affirmations.** Brief affirmations can be used in meditation. My favorites include "God is within me" and "I love myself."

Some people think meditation takes time *away* from physical accomplishment. Taken to extremes, of course, that's true. Most people, however, find that meditation *creates* more time than it *takes.* Meditation is for rest, healing, balance, and information. All these are helpful to attain a goal.

One of the primary complaints people have about meditating is, "My thoughts won't leave me alone." Well *naturally*—that's what the mind does; it *thinks.* Rather than fight the thoughts (good luck), you might *listen* to the thoughts for nuggets

> *This art of resting the mind*
> *and the power*
> *of dismissing from it*
> *all care and worry*
> *is probably*
> *one of the secrets of energy*
> *in our great men.*
>
> CAPTAIN J. A. HADFIELD

of information. If a thought reminds you of something to do, write it down (or record it on a tape recorder). Then return to the meditation.

As the "to do" list fills, the mind empties. If the thought, "Call the bank," reappears, you need only tell yourself, "It's on the list. I can let that one go." And you will. It is important, however, to *do* the things on the list—or at least in a nonmeditative state to consider doing them. If you don't, you will continue to think about them, again and again.

When finished meditating, not only will you have had a better meditation, you will also have a "to do" list that can be very useful. One insight gleaned during a few minutes of meditation might save *hours*, perhaps *days* of unnecessary work. That's what I mean when I say—from a purely practical point of view—meditation can make more time than it takes.

*First keep the peace*
*within yourself,*
*then you can also*
*bring peace to others.*

THOMAS À KEMPIS

1420

# Peace

If you want peace, stop fighting.

If you want peace of mind, stop fighting with your thoughts. Let them be. Let your mind think what it wants to think. It's going to anyway. As long as your mind gives you enough focus to take the next step in the direction you want to go, then let it be.

If you want peace in your emotions, stop trying to control them. Emotions are there to feel. Feel them. Take information from them as needed., and let them be what they want.

If you want physical peace, stop struggling. Don't push your body beyond its fatigue point. Get enough rest and exercise. Let your body be. Don't demand that it live up to every image of performance and perfection you *think* it should have.

If you want peace with others, don't fight them. Go your own way. Live your own life. If some walk with you, fine. If you walk alone for a while, fine. If you don't like what's going on somewhere, leave. Maintain a portable paradise within yourself.

This does not mean you have to *like* what's going on. "The lion shall lie down with the lamb." It does not say the lion shall *make love* to the lamb. If you know you have to lie down with the lamb, bring a good book. That will occupy your mind so you don't have to feel animosity toward the lamb— you don't have to think about the lamb at all.

(And if you're the lamb, don't forget to wear

> *Nothing can bring you peace*
> *but yourself.*
>
> EMERSON

your chain-mail fleece.)

When you're not against yourself or others, you are at peace.

*We shall find peace.*
*We shall hear the angels,*
*we shall see the sky*
*sparkling with diamonds.*

CHEKHOV

1897

*Fortunate, indeed, is*
*the man who takes*
*exactly the right*
*measure of himself,*
*and holds a just balance between*
*what he can acquire*
*and*
*what he can use,*
*be it great or be it small!*

PETER LATHAM

1789–1875

# Balance

Have you noticed some contradictions in this book? So have I. Welcome to life.

Should we "get off our buts" and "do it," or should we "meditate, contemplate, and just sits." Should we laugh or cry? Should we work for money or for wealth? Should we cling tight to this life, or should we look forward to the release of death? Should we be flexible or firm? Assertive or accepting? Giving or receiving?

There is no single answer to these questions. It's a matter of time and timing, of seas and seasons, of breathing in and breathing out.

It's a matter of balance.

Balance is the point between the extremes. But it's not a static point—"I've found it; this is it!" The point is always shifting, always moving. A successful life can be like a successful tightrope walk. Sometimes the balance pole dips violently one way, sometimes it dips gently the other, and sometimes it's perfectly still.

How does one find and maintain balance? Vigilance. Internal vigilance. Internal vigilance is the price of freedom.

When you notice yourself out-of-balance, balance it at once. If you don't, it will find a reflection outside. Then there's something "out there" to balance, too. It's easier to balance it within, before it gets out.

For balanced action, ask yourself, "What would

> *The art of progress*
> *is to preserve order*
> *amid change*
> *and to preserve change*
> *amid order.*
>
> ALFRED NORTH WHITEHEAD

a master do?" Look through the eyes of a master. Masters always perform "right action." Seeing as a master sees, ask yourself, "What would a master do?" Sometimes a master would do nothing. Sometimes, quite a lot. "What would a master do?" Do that.

You are a master. You may as well get good at it.

*This . . . reminds me of the way*
*they used to weigh hogs in Texas.*
*They would get a long plank,*
*put it over a cross-bar,*
*and somehow tie the hog*
*on one end of the plank.*
*They'd search all around*
*till they found a stone*
*that would balance the weight of the hog*
*and they'd put that*
*on the other end of the plank.*
*Then they'd guess the weight of the stone.*

JOHN DEWEY

*People think*
*love is an emotion.*
*Love is good sense.*

KEN KESEY

# Loving

When we go within, we know that our core—our very being—is love. All we can do is share that love with ourselves and others; to make it a verb and to love as much as we can.

Our loving is a work in progress. We are continuously refining it, honing it, adding to it, shaping it. This is what we *think* we are doing. We also know love is continuously refining, honing, adding to, and shaping *us*.

Writing this book was an act of loving. I wanted to communicate the ideas found here because I find these ideas valuable. I know that reading this book was an act of loving on your part. People do not read books such as this without a fierce commitment to the love of self and others.

I wish I knew how to end this book. I am certainly capable of serving up some platitudes on love and calling it a day. But I've been honest with you thus far. I've written from my experiences—from my heart to yours, I like to think.

What *do* I have to say about loving?

- *Loving* is an action. *Love* is a feeling. The difference between love and loving, is the difference between fish and fishing. I like *loving*—the moving, growing, changing, active, dynamic interplay (inner play?) between self and others, and between self and self.

> *If you feel you have*
> *both feet planted*
> *on level ground,*
> *then the university*
> *has failed you.*
>
> ROBERT F. GOHEEN

- Loving starts with the individual. When we want loving from someone else to "make us whole," we know we are not giving ourselves the loving we need.

- When we give ourselves the loving we need (and it takes so little time when we actually *do* it), our time with others tends to be joyful, graceful, playful, touching—in each moment complete.

- Loving is the greatest teacher.

≈

This book cannot be wrapped up in string and handed to you as a tidy package. Neither can life. Or loving. Life is a process. Ongoing processes don't have tidy endings, merely transitions.

So welcome to the transitional chapter of this book. From this point, it's not a book to be *read* (you're within minutes of completing that), but a book to be *used*.

And I, to the degree that I have been a "teacher," gladly hand the mantle over to your Master Teacher. I am content to become a reference librarian—here when you need to research questions such as "How am I supposed to use guilt as a friend?" "What was this about using relationships as a mirror?" or "Didn't he say something about *money?*"

At this point, I step down from the lectern and join you as a classmate.

It's been good taking this journey with you. Thank you for joining me—and letting me join you. *LIFE 101* now makes the transition from a book that leads, to a book you can carry.

Take good care. School is still in session. The surprise continues.

Enjoy.

*Your vision
will become clear
only when you can look
into your own heart.
Who looks outside, dreams;
who looks inside, awakes.*

CARL JUNG

*Gude nicht, and joy be wi' you a'.*

CAROLINA OLIPHANT

*LIFE AND SONGS*

1869

A NEW EDITION
COMPLETELY REVISED

#1 BEST SELLER

# DO IT!
## Let's Get Off Our Buts

IMPORTANT MESSAGE

A GUIDE TO LIVING YOUR DREAMS

## Peter McWilliams

| #1 BESTSELLER | FOLLOW | TERRIFIC |
|---|---|---|
| —New York Times | YOUR DREAMS | —Larry King |
| | —Detroit News | |

**PAPERBACK**
4x7, 494 pages, $5.95
ISBN: 0-931580-79-X

*NEW RECORDING!*

**AUDIO TAPES**
*Presented by the author*
Eight cassettes, $24.95
ISBN: 0-931580-15-3
Available September 1995

# INTRODUCTION:
# How Do You Do?

We all have a dream, a heart's desire. Most have more than one. Some of us have an entire entourage. This is a book about discovering (or rediscovering) those dreams, how to choose which dreams to pursue, and practical suggestions for achieving them.

- By pursuing any *one* of our dreams, we can find fulfillment. We don't need to pursue them all.

- We don't have to *achieve* a dream in order to find fulfillment—we need only actively *pursue* the dream to attain satisfaction.

- By living our dream, we can contribute not only to ourselves, but to everyone and everything around us.

And yet, with all this good news, most people are not pursuing their dreams.

When we're not pursuing our dreams, we spend our time and abilities pursuing the things we *think* will make us happy, the things we *believe* will bring us fulfillment: the house, the car, the cashmere jump suit.

There's an old saying: "You can't get enough of what you don't really want." When the new car doesn't make us happy, we tend to blame the new car for not being "enough," and set our sights on a "better" new car. Surely *that* will make us happy.

> *I stopped believing in Santa Claus*
> *when my mother took me to*
> *see him in a department store,*
> *and he asked for my autograph.*
>
> SHIRLEY TEMPLE

Many people are so far away from living their dream *they have forgotten what their dream truly is.*

It is sad. It is unnecessary. It is wasteful. We have abandoned our heart's desire—and somewhere, deep down, we know it. Even if we don't remember quite what it is—we miss it.

Why aren't we living our dreams?

Because there is something we are trained to honor more than our dreams: the comfort zone. The comfort zone is all the things we have done often enough to feel comfortable doing again.

Whenever we do something new, it falls outside the barrier of the comfort zone. In even *contemplating* a new action, we feel fear, guilt, unworthiness, hurt feelings, and/or anger—all those

Excerpt from *DO IT! Let's Get Off Our Buts*

things we generally think of as "uncomfortable."

When we feel uncomfortable enough long enough, we tend to feel discouraged (a form of exhaustion), and we return to thoughts, feelings and actions that are more familiar, more practiced, more predictable—more, well, *comfortable.*

The irony is that the feelings we have been taught to label "uncomfortable" are, in fact, among the very tools necessary to fulfill our dreams.

As it turns out, the bricks used to build the walls of comfort zone are made of gold.

Why don't we know this?

The training we received as children—which, for the most part, is fine for children—is not appropriate for adults. The guidelines of an independent, productive adult are not the same rules of a dependent, limited child. What is true for children can be counterproductive for adults. We live our lives as though it were a bicycle with the training wheels still on—limiting, entirely *too* safe, and somewhat boring.

We no longer believe in Santa Claus, but we still believe that "being uncomfortable" is reason enough not to do something new. The Easter Bunny hopped out of our lives years ago, yet we still let "what other people might think" affect our behavior. The tooth fairy was yanked from us long before adolescence, but we still feel we can justify any personal failure by finding someone or something outside ourselves to blame.

Most people are drifting along in a childish sleep. To live our dreams, we must wake up.

> *Regret for the things we did*
> *can be tempered by time;*
> *it is regret for the things we*
> *did not do that is inconsolable.*
>
> SYDNEY J. HARRIS

In reading that last sentence, do you feel your comfort zone being challenged? That will happen a lot in this book. That tingling we feel when we contemplate waking up and living our dreams we can label either "fear" or "excitement." If we call it fear, it's uncomfortable; we tend to find reasons not to read any further. If we call it excitement, we turn it into energy that makes the process of learning and doing active and enjoyable.

It's your choice. It's always your choice. Alas, many of us have delegated the choice to habits formed long ago, formed when we knew far less about life than we know now. We let habits formed when we were two or four or six or ten or fifteen control our lives today.

Excerpt from *DO IT! Let's Get Off Our Buts*

To change a habit requires work. Make no mistake about it: reading this book will not change your life, just as reading a guidebook to France will not show you France. It may give you a *sense* of France, perhaps, but France is France and can only be experienced through *action*.

And so it is with your dreams. This book will show you *how* to discover your dreams, *how* to select the dreams you choose to pursue, and *how* to fulfill those dreams—but if you don't *act* upon those *how's*, you will never see Paris from atop the Eiffel Tower.

Although fulfilling our dreams requires *work*, the process can also be *fun*. Which reminds me of a joke.

An Indian Chief greeted a friend by raising his hand in the traditional salute and saying, "Chance!"

"Chance?" his friend asked, "You must mean 'How!'"

"I know how," the Chief responded, "I'm looking for chance."

Please think of this book as your chance— a chance *you* are giving *yourself.* Imagine for a moment that you are powerful enough to have had this book written *just for you.* When you get a sense of that power, you'll know that you have all it takes to fulfill your dream. *Any* dream. *Your* dream.

F. Scott Fitzgerald met Joan Crawford at a Hollywood party. He told her he had been hired to write the screenplay for her next film. She looked

> *Do not be too timid*
> *and squeamish*
> *about your actions.*
> *All life is an experiment.*
>
> RALPH WALDO EMERSON

him straight in the eye and said, "Write hard, Mr. Fitzgerald, write hard."

Imagine that I am looking you straight in the eye and saying, "Dream big, dear reader, dream big."

When we discover how easy it is to fulfill personal dreams—even the ones that seem "really big" before the achievement of them—we are naturally inspired to fulfill even larger dreams.

Pursuing a Big Dream of your own choosing is the same amount of work as gathering more and more of the things you don't really want. You're going to spend the rest of your life doing *something*. It might as well be something *you* want to do.

"But what about money? But what about time? But what about this? But what about that?" There *are* a lot of buts to "get off," aren't there?

Let's return to the question I posed earlier: "How do you do?"

That's easy. You do by learning.

And how do you learn?

You learn by doing.

A chicken-and-egg conundrum, to be sure; yet one penetrated by this deceptively simple thought: "The willingness to do creates the ability to do."

For now, simply be *willing* to do. Be willing to do what it takes to read this book. That takes the willingness to finish this page and turn to the next. That takes the willingness to finish this paragraph. That takes the willingness to finish this sentence (which you have just done—congratulations!).

Where does the willingness come from?

From you.

As Joni Mitchell pointed out, "It all comes down to you."

I certainly agree, and would only add, "It all comes down to *do*."

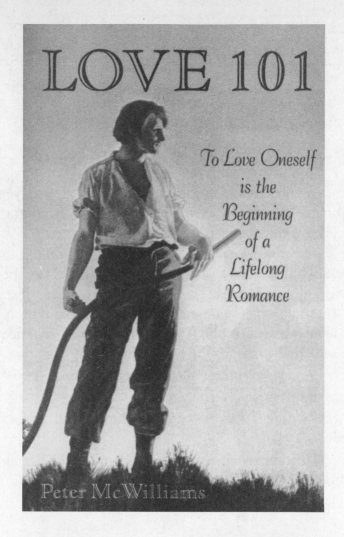

**LOVE 101**

*To Love Oneself
is the
Beginning
of a
Lifelong
Romance*

Peter McWilliams

TRADE PAPERBACK
5x8, 448 pages, $11.95
ISBN: 0-931580-70-6

AUDIO TAPES
*Presented by the author
with old songs and lots of fun!*
Eight tapes
Unabridged, $24.95
ISBN: 0-931580-71-4

*Definitely NOT
just "your basic
book-on-tape"*

# Author's Notes

In the early 1970s, I went to the American Booksellers Association annual convention, where publishers rent booths at exorbitant rates and show their recent wares to the booksellers of America. At the Penguin booth, I saw a book entitled *Self Love*. It had an introduction by Alan Watts, who was then and is still my favorite philosopher. I was excited to discover a book about the love of oneself endorsed by him and published by such a distinguished house as Penguin—then known primarily for its reprints of the classics. As was the custom at ABA, complimentary copies were available. I took my copy and thanked the salesperson, a dignified British man who nodded his acceptance of my appreciation.

"I can really use this book," I said. "I'm very bad at self-love."

The sales representative smiled one of those smiles that doesn't go up at the edges, but merely makes one's mouth wider while perfectly horizontal.

"In fact, of all the things I need to work on," I continued, "I think self-love is the most essential." I was twenty-something at the time, and determined to be "open about my process." I could see, however, that saying I didn't know how to love myself made the Penguin sales representative a bit uncomfortable, so I said my good-bye.

"Thank you again," I said, extending my hand. As he shook it, I said, "In fact, I'm going up to my hotel room right now and read this." He dropped my hand.

The Penguin book on self-love was about the joys of masturbation.

---

> *The last time I saw him*
> *he was walking down Lover's Lane*
> *holding his own hand.*
>
> FRED ALLEN

My seeking self-love in the early 1970s was sincere. Like many people, I had inhaled the book *How to Be Your Own Best Friend*. I read it clandestinely—it seemed to be as taboo a subject as that *other* form of self-love. In 1971, the idea that one could be one's own friend, much less *best* friend, was radical.

Today, the notion that one can be the most significant love object in one's own life, is just as radical.

I certainly do not present myself as a pillar of self-loving, nor put myself on a pedestal labeled AN IDEAL SPECIMEN OF A SELF-LOVING PERSON. I'm just a person who has been struggling with the notion of loving himself since 1967. Twenty-eight years later, I finally feel as though I have *something* worth sharing; that I know enough about the subject to write a book on it; and, since there's something more to learn about everything, "The best way to learn about a subject," Benjamin Disraeli once said, "is to write a book about it."

Although your path and discoveries on the road to greater self-love will differ from mine, allow me to offer three personal observations:

1. God* is within you.**

2. You are lovable, *just as you are now.*

3. You *can* learn to love yourself, more and more each day.

In this book I will not be spending a great deal of time on point #1. The discovery of, defining of, relating to, and praise for God I will leave to you, God, and any number of excellent source materials on the subject. *LOVE 101* can be read by anyone, from devout fundamentalist to confirmed atheist, and he or she can learn enough about self-loving to proclaim, "Glory, hallelujah! I'm glad I read this book."

In the end, of course, we must all write our own book on how to love ourselves. Thanks for reading my

*As you perceive him, her, or it to be, from God the Father, to Mother Nature, to Universal Mind, to the "illimitable superior spirit who reveals himself in the slight details we are able to perceive with our frail and feeble mind" (Einstein).

**For those who find this an anti-Christian statement, please consider this from Jesus: "The kingdom of God is within you" (Luke 17:21).

> *Style is knowing who you are,*
> *what you want to say,*
> *and not giving a damn.*
>
> GORE VIDAL

book. My best and warmest wishes to you as you write your own.

Take good care,

> Peter McWilliams
> Los Angeles, California
> January 3, 1995

P.S. *LOVE 101: To Love Oneself Is the Beginning of a Life-long Romance* was completed on January 3, 1995. Precisely one hundred years earlier—to the day—the curtain rose at London's Theatre Royal on Oscar Wilde's latest play, *An Ideal Husband*. As the third act opens, we find this stage direction:

*Enter* LORD GORING *in evening dress with a button hole [flower in his lapel]. He is wearing a silk hat and Inverness cape. White-gloved, he carries a Louis Seize cane. His are all the delicate fopperies of fashion. One sees that he stands in immediate relation to modern life, makes it, indeed, and so masters it. He is the first well-dressed philosopher in the history of thought.*

Could Wilde possibly be describing himself? But of course. Goring addresses his butler:

LORD GORING: You see, Phipps, fashion is what one wears oneself. Whereas unfashionable is what other people wear.

PHIPPS: Yes, my lord.

LORD GORING: Just as vulgarity is simply the conduct of other people.

PHIPPS: Yes, my lord.

LORD GORING [putting in new button hole]: And falsehoods the truths of other people.

PHIPPS: Yes, my lord.

LORD GORING: To love oneself is the beginning of a lifelong romance.

PHIPPS: Yes, my lord.

And from that bit of typical Wilde dialogue comes the subtitle for this book.

*To fall in love
with yourself
is the first secret
of happiness.*

*I did so at the age
of four-and-a-half.*

*Then if you're not
a good mixer
you can always
fall back on
your own company.*

ROBERT MORLEY

# INTRODUCTION:
# You Are Already Living
# with the Love of Your Life

This is a book about a myth and a taboo.

THE MYTH: In order to be complete and fulfilled, you must find one "significant other" to love. This significant other must consider you his or her significant other and love you back with equal devotion till death do you part.

THE TABOO: It is somehow unwholesome to love yourself.

In *LOVE 101* I'll be challenging both the myth and the taboo. If you're not ready to have these challenged, it would be best if you stop reading now—this book will only upset you.

If, on the other hand, you have been gradually coming to the seemingly forbidden conclusion that before we can truly love another, or allow another to properly love us, we must first learn to love ourselves—then this book is for you.

The taboo that we shouldn't love ourselves is one of the silliest in modern culture. Who else is more qualified to love you than you? Who else knows what you want, precisely when you want it, and is always around to supply it?

Who do you go to bed with, sleep with, dream with, shower with, eat with, work with, play with, pray with, go to the movies with, and watch TV with?

---

Excerpt from *LOVE 101*

> *The continued propinquity*
> *of another human being*
> *cramps your style after a time*
> *unless that person*
> *is somebody you think you love.*
>
> *Then the burden*
> *becomes intolerable at once.*
>
> QUENTIN CRISP

Who else knows where it itches, and just how hard to scratch it?

Who are you reading this book with?

Who have you always lived with, and whom will you eventually die with?

And, who will be the only person to accompany you on that ultimate adventure (just think of death as a theme park with a high admission cost), while all your *other* loved ones are consoling each other by saying how happy you must be with God and how natural you look?

Spiritually, who is the only person who can join you in your relationship with God, Jesus, Buddha, Mohammed, Moses, Mother Nature, The Force, Creative

Excerpt from *LOVE 101*

Intelligence, or whomever or whatever you consider to be the moving force of existence?

And, who has been there every time you've had sex?*

So, from the sacred to the profane (and all points in between), your ideal lover is *you*.

Then why is loving ourselves such a taboo? Why is the notion that we *need* another to love (who will love us back) such an enormous myth?

In a word, control.

The self-contained, emotionally autonomous, intellectually free individual is the greatest threat to the institutions that want to control us. Those of us who refuse to act like sheep—who question authority and want genuine answers, not just knee-jerk clichés—are a pain in the *gluteus maximus* (and regions nearby) to those who want to rule by *power* rather than by providing *leadership*.

We see attempts to manipulate almost everywhere—in politics, religion, advertising, entertainment.

When we are programmed to "fall" for the hunk or the honey of a certain aesthetic type, and to believe that these images of sex and beauty mean "true love," then these images can be used to sell us anything from cigarettes to movie tickets. And they are, they are.

*Yes, from time to time others may have been nearby doing what they could to help, but whatever pleasure you felt was inside yourself, experienced in those inner electrochemical, physiological pleasure places that are entirely your own. This is true for *anything* pleasurable we see, feel, hear, touch, or taste: without *our senses* nothing "out there"—from movies to pepperoni pizza—would be in the least enjoyable.

> *Conformity*
> *is the jailer of freedom*
> *and the enemy of growth.*
>
> JOHN F. KENNEDY

Further, when the only "moral" outcome of a romantic relationship is a till-death-do-us-part, state-licensed, church-blessed marriage, we see the fundamental forces of conformity at work. If we're all the *same,* we are much easier to *serve*—also sell to, also control.

If we're all the same—and marriage is one of the best homogenizers around—then we only need one religion, one political party: the Family Values Party. In fact, why not combine religion and government in one?

That's been the history of the world—church and state hand-in-hand, slavish conformity, and those troublemakers (ungodly and unpatriotic) who fail to shape up . . . well, there have always been ways of dealing with *them.*

But this book is not a political diatribe. It's a book about personal freedom—the freedom to choose the life you want, even though the powers that be think you should not do so. They know best.

Except they don't. More than half the people in this country live outside the "traditional" mama-papa-children household. It hasn't worked.

Please understand that I am not against family, marriage, children, or even romance. I am merely against the idea that we should *all* be herded into that mode of relating when there are viable, satisfying alternatives (which we'll explore later in this book).

There will always be people who want to get married and raise children. More power to them. The trouble arises when people who want to do something *else* (write, pray, save the dolphins) get married and have children because they think they *should,* not because they *want to.*

This clutters up the marriage market with unqualified players—those who would rather be training for a decathlon just don't have the same *commitment* to childrearing. So, they drop out of the marriage—emotionally or entirely—and the other partner, who still *wants* a marriage, wonders, "What happened?"

What happened is what happens every time we are all programmed to do the same thing—those who don't really want to be there muck it up for those who do.

If a group of people were all taken to an opera one night, a rock concert the second night, the latest Woody Allen movie the third night, and an Englebert Humperdink concert the fourth, chances are that on at least one

> *Mass democracy, mass morality*
> *and the mass media thrive*
> *independently of the individual,*
> *who joins them only at the cost*
> *of at least a partial perversion*
> *of his instinct and insights.*
>
> *He pays for his social ease*
> *with what used to be called his soul,*
> *his discriminations, his uniqueness,*
> *his psychic energy, his self.*
>
> AL ALVAREZ

of those nights, some of the audience would be, to paraphrase S. J. Pearlman, if not disgruntled, certainly not fully gruntled.

If, on the other hand, each individual in the group had a choice to go to any, all, or none of the four, then self-selection would lead to far more gruntled audiences at *all* the events.

This book is about you getting more gruntled in *all* your relationships—especially your relationship with yourself.

You'll note I've only talked about the failure of marriage. Imagine how much more unsuccessful romance is. There are two million divorces in the United States each year. Is it fair to estimate that for every divorce there are at least ten break-ups between nonmarried romantics? If so, there are, counting the newly divorced, twenty-two million broken hearts littering the emotional landscape. There are also twenty-two million (the ones who did the dumping) who are proclaiming "Free at last!"

And yet the majority of those millions, who now have already had first-hand experience that a romantic relationship doesn't necessarily lead to a lifelong happy marriage, will *again* be jumping into the next acceptable pair of eyes, or thighs, that come along. "The *person* was the problem," they tell themselves. "If only I find the right *person*." Maybe it's the *type of relationship* that's not working. Maybe.

What does it cost us to fall for this myth that we must find another to love, and must (in the same person) find someone to love us? It costs us the loving, laughing, emotionally stable, intellectually stimulating, and physically satisfying relationship with the person perfectly qualified to be our best friend in this lifetime—ourselves.

We trade the ongoing, here-and-now, potentially vibrant, fun-filled, nurturing relationship with ourselves for some future promise of Prince Charming or Cinderella riding in on a white charger or a refurbished pumpkin, transforming our lives with True Love. That's like not eating your home-cooked food because you have been convinced that any day now (real soon), a gourmet (not just any gourmet, mind you, but your own personal star-crossed gourmet) will appear—pots, pans, leeks, and all.

Am I saying you should turn the gourmet away?

> *Love, love, love—all the wretched cant
> of it, masking egotism, lust, maso-
> chism, fantasy under a mythology of
> sentimental postures, a welter of self
> induced miseries and joys, blinding
> and masking the essential personalities
> in the frozen gestures of courtship, in
> the kissing and the dating and the
> desire, the compliments and the
> quarrels which vivify its barrenness.*
>
> GERMAINE GREER

Not *at all*. Being with others, sharing with others, supporting and being supported by others are among the
most fulfilling activities we can enjoy. I'm simply saying
that loving oneself *while* loving others makes *all* interac-
tions more enjoyable.

Some even say that loving oneself is a *prerequisite* to
loving others. I won't take it quite that far, but I do
know loving oneself is an *important* part of loving others (and allowing others to love you).

When we are already loving and loved by ourselves, our desire to love and be loved by others is just
that—a desire. We no longer have the burning, aching
*need* to love and be loved. Back in my desperately seek-
ing-another-to-love-who-will-love-me-back days, I wrote
a poem:

Excerpt from *LOVE 101*

My needs destroy
the paths
through which
those needs
could be
fulfilled.

I had on my wall in letters a foot tall, the needy proclamation taken from Peter Townsend's *Tommy:*

SEE ME

FEEL ME

TOUCH ME

HEAL ME

Talk about an *intimidating* message to present to the newly met.

At seventeen, my muse gave me the answer. I was sitting in a coffee shop as the sun was coming up and wrote on a paper napkin (as all poets do from time to time):

I must conquer my loneliness
alone.

I must be happy with myself
or I have
nothing
to offer.

Two halves have
little choice
but to
join,
and yes,
they do
make a
whole.

*I am two fools, I know,*
*For loving, and for saying so*
*In whining poetry*

JOHN DONNE
1572–1631

But two
wholes,
when they coincide . . .

that is
beauty.

That is
love.

It took me some time—with any number of false
starts, dead ends, and dashed hopes*—to get the wisdom of this edict off the napkin and into my life.

*LOVE 101* is what I learned along the way. You may
have a different way with different learnings, but I pray

---

*But I did sell a large pile of poetry books along the way!
When life gives you lemons, write *The Lemon Cookbook.*

that some of my musings you'll find useful, inspiring, or amusing.

I wrote this book for myself—a collection of what I have learned about self-loving so that if I fall into a pit of self-loathing (an inevitability—what lovers don't have quarrels?), I will have these reminders to help me de-pit myself.

I hope you'll read along in my "manual on loving me" and make as much of it your own as you care to.

# Introduction

This is not just a book for people with life-threatening illnesses. It's a book for anyone afflicted with one of the primary diseases of our time: negative thinking.

I come before you a certified expert on the subject: I'm a confirmed negaholic. I don't just see a glass that's half-full and call it half-empty; I see a glass that's completely full and worry that someone's going to tip it over.

Negative thinking is always expensive—dragging us down mentally, emotionally, and physically—hence, I refer to any indulgence in it as a *luxury*. When, however, we have the symptoms of a life-threatening illness—be it AIDS, heart trouble, cancer, high blood pressure, or any of the others—negative thinking is a *luxury* we can no longer afford.

I remember a bumper sticker from the 1960s—"Death Is Nature's Way of Telling You to Slow Down." Well, the signs of a life-threatening illness are nature's way of telling us to—as we say in California—lighten up.

Be easier on yourself. Think better of yourself. Learn to forgive yourself and others.

This is a book about getting behind on your worrying. Way, way behind. The further behind on your worrying you get, the further ahead you'll be.

My favorite quote on worry: "Worrying is a form of atheism." Second favorite: "Worrying is the interest paid on a debt you may not owe."

> *We are, perhaps,*
> *unique among the*
> *earth's creatures,*
> *the worrying animal.*
> *We worry away our lives,*
> *fearing the future,*
> *discontent with the present,*
> *unable to take in*
> *the idea of dying,*
> *unable to sit still.*
>
> LEWIS THOMAS

This is not so much a book to be read as it is a book to be *used*. It doesn't have to be read cover to cover. I like to think you can flip it open at any time to any page and get something of value from it. This is especially true of the second—and longest—section of the book.

This book has two sections: **The Disease** and **The Cure.**

The disease is not any specific illness, but what I believe to be a precursor of all life-threatening illnesses—negative thinking.

The cure is not a wonder drug or a vaccination or The Magic Bullet. The cure is simple: (1) spend more time focusing on the positive things in your

Excerpt from *You Can't Afford the Luxury of a Negative Thought*

life *(Accentuate the Positive);* (2) spend less time thinking negatively *(Eliminate the Negative);* and (3) enjoy each moment *(Latch on to the Affirmative).*

That's it. Simple, but far from easy.

It's the aim of this book to make the process simple and, if not easy, at least easier.

Please don't use anything in this book against yourself. Don't interpret anything I say in **The Disease** as blame. When I use the word *responsibility,* for example, I simply mean you have the *ability* to *respond.* (And you *are* responding or you wouldn't be reading this book.)

And please don't take any of the suggestions in **The Cure** as "musts," "shoulds," or "have-tos." Think of them as joyful activity, creative play, curious exploration—not as additional burdens in an already burdensome life.

This book is not designed to replace proper medical care. Please use this book *in conjunction with* whatever course of treatment your doctor or health-care provider prescribes.

You are far more powerful than you ever dreamed. As you discover and learn how to use your power, use it only for your upliftment and the upliftment of others.

You are a marvelous, wonderful, worthwhile person—just because you are. That's the point of view I'll be taking. Please join me for a while—an hour, a week, a lifetime—at that viewing point.

As featured on OPRAH!
2,000,000 COPIES IN PRINT

# How to Survive the Loss of a Love

♥ ♥ ♥ ♥   ♥

MELBA COLGROVE, PH.D.
HAROLD H. BLOOMFIELD, M.D.
& PETER McWILLIAMS

**HARDCOVER**
5½x8½, 212 pages, $10.00
ISBN: 0-931580-45-5

**PAPERBACK**
4x7, 212 pages, $5.95
ISBN: 0-931580-43-9

**AUDIO TAPES**
*Read by the authors*
Two cassettes, $11.95
ISBN: 0-931580-47-1

**WORKBOOK**
*Surviving, Healing & Growing*
7x10, 198 pages, $11.95
ISBN: 0-931580-46-3

*When an emotional injury takes place,*
*the body begins a process*
*as natural as the healing*
*of a physical wound.*

*Let the process happen.*
*Trust the process.*
*Surrender to it.*

*Trust that nature will do the healing.*
*Know that the pain will pass,*
*and, when it passes,*
*you will be stronger,*
*happier, more sensitive and aware.*

---

Excerpt from *How to Survive the Loss of a Love*

# THE STAGES OF RECOVERY

- Recovering from a loss takes place in three distinct—yet overlapping—stages.

- They are:

    —shock/denial/numbness
    —fear/anger/depression
    —understanding/acceptance/moving on

- Each stage of recovery is:

    —necessary
    —natural
    —a part of the healing process

Excerpt from *How to Survive the Loss of a Love*

*the fear that I would*
*come home one day and*
*find you gone has turned*
*into the pain of the*
*reality.*

*"What will I do if it happens?"*
*I would ask myself.*

*What will I do*
*now that it*
*has?*

## *One:*
## You Will Survive

- You *will* get better.

- No doubt about it.

- The healing process has a beginning, a middle, and an end.

- Keep in mind, at the beginning, that there *is* an end. It's not that far off. You *will* heal.

- Nature is on your side, and nature is a powerful ally.

- Tell yourself, often, "I am alive. I will survive."

- You are alive.

- You will survive.

*in my sleep*
*I dreamed*
*you called. you said*
*you were moving back*
*with your old lover.*
*you said you thought a*
*phone call would be the*
*cleanest way to handle it,*
*"it" being that we could*
*never see each other*
*again, and that I should*
*understand why.*
*I moved to wake*
*myself and found I wasn't*
*sleeping after all.*
*my life became*
*a nightmare.*

*Five:*
# It's OK to Feel

- It's OK to feel numb. Expect to be in shock for awhile. This emotional numbness may be frightening.

- It's OK to fear. "Will I make it?" "Will I ever love again?" "Will I ever feel good about anything again?" These are familiar fears following a loss. It's OK to *feel* them, but, to the degree you can, don't *believe* them.

- It's OK to feel nothing. There are times when you'll have no feelings of any kind. That's fine.

- It's OK to feel anything. You may feel grief-stricken, angry, like a failure, exhausted, muddled, lost, beaten, indecisive, relieved, overwhelmed, inferior, melancholy, giddy, silly, loathful, full of self-hatred, envious, suicidal (feelings OK, actions not), disgusted, happy, outraged, in rage or *anything* else.

- *All* feelings are a part of the healing process.

- Let yourself heal. Let yourself feel.

*Spring:*
*leaves grow.*
*love grows.*

*Summer:*
*love dies.*
*I drive away,*
*tears in my eyes.*

*Bugs commit suicide on my windshield.*

*Autumn:*
*leaves fall.*
*I fall.*

*Winter:*
*I die.*
*I drive away,*
*nothing in my eyes.*

*Snowflakes commit suicide on my windshield.*

# *Seven:*
# You're Great!

- You are a good, whole, worthwhile human being.

- You are OK. You're more than OK, you're great.

- Your self-esteem may have suffered a jolt. Your thoughts may reflect some guilt, worry, condemnation or self-deprecation. These thoughts are just symptoms of the stress you are going through.

- There is no need to give negative thoughts about yourself the center of attention.

- Don't punish yourself with "if only's." (*"If only* I had [or hadn't] done this or that I wouldn't be in this emotional mess.") Disregard any thought that begins "If only . . ."

- You are much more than the emotional wound you are currently suffering. Don't lose sight of that.

- Beneath the surface turmoil:

  —you are good
  —you are whole
  —you are beautiful

  just because you are

---

Excerpt from *How to Survive the Loss of a Love*

*I am Joy.*
*I am everything.*
*I can do all things but two:*

*1. forget that I love you.*

*2. forget that you no longer love me.*

## Twenty-five:
# The Question of Suicide

- You may be having suicidal thoughts. They may or may not be as eloquent as *"to be or not to be,"* but they may arise.

- Know they are a natural symptom of the pain, and that there is no need to act on them.

- If you fear these impulses are getting out of hand, seek professional help *at once.* Call directory assistance and ask for the number of your local Suicide Prevention Hotline. Then call it. The people (almost entirely volunteers) are there to help. They *want* to help. Give them the gift of allowing them to do so.

- Don't turn the rage against yourself. (Although feeling rage is perfectly alright—after all, an utterly outrageous thing has happened to you.) Find a safe way to release it. Beat a pillow, cry, scream, stomp up and down, yell.

- Above all, suicide is silly. It's leaving the world series ten minutes into the first inning just because your favorite hitter struck out. It's walking out of the opera during the overture just because the conductor dropped his baton. It's . . . well, you get the picture. In this play called life, aren't you even a little curious about what might happen next?

- The feeling *will pass.* You can count on that. You *will* get better. *Much* better.

- We do promise you a rose garden. We just can't promise you it will be totally without thorns.

# THE QUESTION OF SUICIDE:

*Keep it a question.*
*it's not really an answer.*

# *Ninety-three:*
## Your Happiness Is Up to You

- Happiness depends on your *attitude* toward what happens to you, not on what happens to you.

- It may sound revolutionary, but problems don't have to make you unhappy.

- This runs counter to our cultural programming—which tells us we *must* react in certain negative ways to certain "negative" events.

- Nonetheless, happiness is always our choice. That is a reality of life.

- Stop waiting for Prince Charming, Cinderella, more money, the right job, total health *or anything else* before you're happy.

- Stop waiting.

- Choose satisfaction.

- Be happy.

- Now.

*I am worthy.*

*I am worthy of my life and
all the good that is in it.*

*I am worthy of
my friends and their friendship.*

*I am worthy of spacious skies, amber waves
of grain and purple mountain majesties
above the fruited plain. (I am worthy, too,
of the fruited plain.)*

*I am worthy of a degree of happiness
that could only be referred to as
"sinful" in less enlightened times.*

*I am worthy of creativity,
sensitivity and appreciation.*

*I am worthy of peace of mind, peace on Earth,
peace in the valley and a piece of the action.*

*I am worthy of God's presence in my life.*

*I am worthy
of my love.*

---

"If you can't remember the last time
you felt genuinely good,
please read this book."
Larry King

# How to
# Heal
# Depression

By the co-authors of
*How to Survive the Loss of a Love*

° Harold H. Bloomfield, M.D.
& Peter McWilliams

**HARDCOVER**
5½x8¼, 240 pages
$14.95
ISBN: 0-931580-34-0

**PAPERBACK**
4x7, 240 pages
$5.95
ISBN: 0-931580-61-7

**AUDIO TAPES**
*Read by the authors*
*(with lots of classic blues songs)*
Six cassettes, $19.95
ISBN: 0-931580-37-4

# Authors' Notes

Welcome.

Our goal is to make this book brief, practical, and to-the-point.

The *last* thing a person with depression wants is an intricate tome, heavy with footnotes, citations, Latin words, and sentences such as "Depression is a biopsychosocial disorder, sometimes treated with monoamine oxidase inhibitors."

We have also included quotes from people, some well known and some not, across many cultures and centuries, to show that depression—and the desire to heal it—is a deeply human and universal experience.

Our approach to the treatment of depression is twofold. Each part is equally important.

- One is healing the brain, as current medical research points to biochemical imbalances in the brain as the seat of depression.

- The other is healing the mind—overcoming negative habits of thought and action which may cause, or be caused by, depression.

Treating the brain *and* the mind is the most effective way to heal depression. Recent medical and psychological breakthroughs make depression among the most successfully treatable of all serious illnesses.

*Harold H. Bloomfield, M.D.*
*Peter McWilliams*

As a confirmed melancholic,
I can testify that the best
and maybe the only antidote
for melancholia is action.
However, like most melancholics,
I also suffer from sloth.

EDWARD ABBEY

Excerpt from *How to Heal Depression*

# About This Book

Our book is divided into four parts.

In Part I, **"Understanding Depression,"** we discuss what depression is (and is not); how you can be depressed without "feeling depressed"; and the possible causes of depression. There's even a short self-evaluation for depression, compliments of the National Institutes of Health (page 22).

In Part II, **"Healing the Brain,"** we look at the biological causes of depression and its medical treatment. This includes antidepressant medication, nutrition, exercise, and such strenuous activities as hot baths and massage. This is the domain of the psychiatrist, family doctor, and other healthcare specialists.

Part III we call **"Healing the Mind."** We explore unlearning mental habits either caused by or contributing to depression, while learning new mental patterns that tend to enhance effectiveness, well-being, and emotional freedom. We discuss exciting new short-term therapies (usually only ten to twenty sessions) that have proven to be highly successful in healing depression. This is the domain of the psychologist, psychiatrist, clinical social worker, and mental health professional.

The final section, Part IV, is **"As Healing Continues . . . ."** Although most people treated for depression find remarkable results within a short time, the complete healing of depression often continues for a while. There are ups and downs, lessons to be learned, new pathways to be explored.

Thank you for joining us on this healing journey.

# One:
# *You Are Not Alone*

- If you or someone you know is depressed, you are not alone.

- *That's* something of an understatement.

- One in twenty Americans currently suffers from a depression severe enough to require medical treatment.

- One person in five will have a depression at some time in his or her life.

- Depression in its various forms (insomnia, fatigue, anxiety, stress, vague aches and pains, etc.) is the most common complaint heard in doctors' offices.

- Two percent of all children and five percent of all adolescents suffer from depression.

- More than twice as many women are currently being treated for depression than men. (It is not known whether this is because women are more likely to be depressed, or whether men tend to deny their depression.)

- People over sixty-five are four times more likely to suffer depression than the rest of the population.

- Depression is the #1 public health problem in this country. Depression is an epidemic—an epidemic on the rise.

Excerpt from *How to Heal Depression*

*I am now experiencing myself*
*all the things that*
*as a third party*
*I have witnessed going on*
*in my patients—*
*days when I slink about*
*depressed.*

SIGMUND FREUD

## Three:
## *There Is No Need to Suffer*

- More than eighty percent of the people with depression can be successfully treated.

- Long-term, expensive treatments are seldom necessary.

- Modern treatment for most depression is antidepressant medication and short-term "talk" therapy—usually just ten to twenty sessions.

- Treatment for depression is relatively inexpensive— but whatever the cost, it is more than made up for in increased productivity, efficiency, physical health, improved relationships, and enjoyment of life.

- Yes, life will always have its "slings and arrows of outrageous fortune," and, yes, they will hurt. But there's no need to suffer from depression as well.

*Pain is inevitable.*
*Suffering is optional.*

M. Kathleen Casey

# Ten:
# *The Symptoms of Depression*

After careful evaluation, the National Institutes of Health developed the following checklist:

**Symptoms of Depression Can Include**
- ☐ Persistent sad or "empty" mood
- ☐ Loss of interest or pleasure in ordinary activities, including sex
- ☐ Decreased energy, fatigue, being "slowed down"
- ☐ Sleep disturbances (insomnia, early-morning waking, or oversleeping)
- ☐ Eating disturbances (loss of appetite and weight, or weight gain)
- ☐ Difficulty concentrating, remembering, making decisions
- ☐ Feelings of guilt, worthlessness, helplessness
- ☐ Thoughts of death or suicide, suicide attempts
- ☐ Irritability
- ☐ Excessive crying
- ☐ Chronic aches and pains that don't respond to treatment

**In the Workplace, Symptoms of Depression Often May Be Recognized by**
- ☐ Decreased productivity
- ☐ Morale problems
- ☐ Lack of cooperation
- ☐ Safety problems, accidents
- ☐ Absenteeism
- ☐ Frequent complaints of being tired all the time
- ☐ Complaints of unexplained aches and pains
- ☐ Alcohol and drug abuse

**Symptoms of Mania Can Include**
- ☐ Excessively "high" mood
- ☐ Irritability
- ☐ Decreased need for sleep
- ☐ Increased energy and activity
- ☐ Increased talking, moving, and sexual activity
- ☐ Racing thoughts
- ☐ Disturbed ability to make decisions
- ☐ Grandiose notions
- ☐ Being easily distracted

Excerpt from *How to Heal Depression*

# Eleven:
# Are You Depressed?

- *"A thorough diagnosis is needed if four or more of the symptoms of depression or mania persist for more than two weeks,"* say the National Institutes of Health, *"or are interfering with work or family life."*

- The symptoms on the facing page are *not* "just life." If four or more of the symptoms have been a regular part of your life for more than two weeks or regularly tend to interfere with your life, a consultation with a physician experienced in diagnosing and treating depression is in order.

- You need not suffer any longer. Treatment is readily available.

- *"With available treatment, eighty percent of the people with serious depression—even those with the most severe forms—can improve significantly,"* say the National Institutes of Health. *"Symptoms can be relieved, usually in a matter of weeks."*

- Please talk to your doctor. (And read on!)

# ABOUT THE AUTHOR

PETER McWILLIAMS has been writing about his passions since 1967. In that year, he became passionate about what most seventeen-year-olds are passionate about—love—and wrote *Come Love With Me & Be My Life*. This began a series of po-etry books which have sold nearly four million copies.

Along with love, of course, comes loss, so Peter became passionate about emotional survival. In 1971 he wrote *Surviving the Loss of a Love*, which was expanded in 1976 and again in 1991 (with co-authors Melba Colgrove, Ph.D., and Harold Bloomfield, M.D.) into *How to Survive the Loss of a Love*. It has sold more than two million copies.

He also became interested in meditation, and a book he wrote on meditation was a *New York Times* bestseller, knocking the impregnable *Joy of Sex* off the #1 spot. As one newspaper headline proclaimed, MEDITATION MORE POPULAR THAN SEX AT THE *NEW YORK TIMES*.

His passion for computers (or, more accurately, for what computers could do) led to *The Personal Computer Book*, which *TIME* proclaimed "a beacon of simplicity, sanity and humor," and the *Wall Street Journal* called "genuinely funny." (Now, really, how many people has the *Wall Street Journal* called "genuinely funny"?)

His passion for personal growth continues in the on-going LIFE 101 SERIES. Thus far, the books in this series include *You Can't Afford the Luxury of a Negative Thought: A Book for People with Any Life-Threatening Illness—Including Life*; *LIFE 101: Everything We Wish We Had Learned About Life In School—But Didn't* (a *New York Times* bestseller in both hardcover and paperback); *DO IT! Let's Get Off Our Buts* (a #1 *New York Times* hardcover bestseller); *WEALTH 101: Wealth Is Much More Than Money*, and *We Give To Love: Giving Is Such a Selfish Thing*.

His passion for visual beauty led him to publish, in 1992, his first book of photography, *PORTRAITS*, a twenty-two-year anthology of his photographic work.

Personal freedom, individual expression, and the right to live one's own life, as long as one does not harm the person or property of another, have long been his passions. He wrote about them in *Ain't Nobody's Business If You Do: The Absurdity of Consensual Crimes in a Free Society*.

After successfully being treated for depression, he wrote with Harold H. Bloomfield, M.D., *How to Heal Depression*.

His fifteen-year sojourn through John-Roger's destructive cult, the Church of the Movement of Spiritual Inner Awareness (MSIA), is documented (with a surprising degree of humor) in *LIFE 102: What to Do When Your Guru Sues You*.

His most recent book is *LOVE 101: To Love Oneself Is the Beginning of a Lifelong Romance*.

All of the above-mentioned books were self-published and are still in print.

Peter McWilliams has appeared on *The Oprah Winfrey Show*, *Larry King* (radio and television), *Donahue*, *Sally Jessy Raphael*, and, a long time ago, the *Regis Philbin Show* (before Regis met Kathie Lee—probably before Kathie Lee was *born*).

# Other Books by Peter McWilliams

### *LIFE 101 Audio Tapes*
The unabridged text of this book, read by the author. **Six cassettes.** $22.95.

### *The Portable LIFE 101*
179 essential excerpts plus 177 quotations from the *New York Times* bestseller *LIFE 101*. Think of it as the Cliff Notes to life. **Trade paperback,** $5.95.

### *DO IT! Let's Get Off Our Buts*
This is a book for those who want to discover—clearly and precisely—their dream; how to pursue that dream, even if it means learning (and—gasp!—practicing) some new behavior; and who wouldn't mind having some fun along the way. 500 pages. **Paperback,** $5.95. **Audio tapes** (unabridged, six cassettes), $24.95

### *DO IT! Audio Tapes*
The unabridged text of this book, read by the author. **Eight cassettes.** $24.95.

### *The Portable DO IT!*
A collection of reminders and quotes to encourage you to continue getting off your buts. The perfect pocket companion on the road to fulfilling your dreams. 208 pages. **Trade paperback,** $5.95.

### *LOVE 101 Loving Oneself is the Beginning of a Lifelong Romance*
If you were arrested for being kind to yourself, would there be enough evidence to convict you? If not, this book (or audio tape set) is a must. It explores improving the most important relationship in your life—your relationship with yourself. After all, you're the only person you'll be eating with, watching TV with, bathing with, and sleeping with for the rest of your life. 400 pages **Trade paperback,** $11.95. **Audio tapes** (unabridged, eight cassettes, includes Meditation tape), $24.95.

### How to Heal Depression
by Harold H. Bloomfield, M.D.,
and Peter McWilliams

The first companion book of the eighteen-year bestseller, *How to Survive the Loss of a Love*. In simple, clear, direct prose (with quotes on every other page) it explains what depression is, what causes it, and what the most effective treatments are. **Hardcover,** $14.95. **Audio tapes** (unabridged, six cassettes, read by the authors), $19.95.

### You Can't Afford the Luxury of a Negative Thought
### A Book for People with Any Life-Threatening illness including Life

This is a book for anyone afflicted with one of the primary diseases of our time: negative thinking. 622 pages. **Paperback,** $5.95. **Audio tapes** (unabridged, eight cassettes), $24.95. **Wristwatch,** $35.00.

### Focus on the Positive

Exercises, processes, journal space, drawing room, and more—all designed to complement the material in the preceding book. 200 pages. **Trade paperback,** $11.95.

### How to Survive the Loss of a Love
by Melba Colgrove, Ph.D., Harold H. Bloomfield, M.D., and Peter McWilliams

A directly helpful guide to recovering from any loss or major change in life. 212 pages. **Hardcover,** $12.95 **Trade paperback** (rack size), $5.95. **Audio tapes** (unabridged, two cassettes, read by the authors), $11.95.

### Surviving, Healing and Growing
#### The How to Survive the Loss of a Love Workbook

Exercises, processes, and suggestions designed to supplement *How to Survive the Loss of a Love*. Lots of room to write, draw, doodle, survive, heal & grow. 200 pages. **Trade paperback,** $11.95.

### Ain't Nobody's Business If You Do
#### The Absurdity of Consensual Crimes in a Free Society

The idea behind this book is simple: As an adult, you should be allowed to do with your person and property whatever you choose, as long as you don't physically harm the person or property of another. 818 pages. **Hardcover,** $11.47. **Paperback,** $5.95.

### LIFE 102:
### *What to Do When Your Guru Sues You*

This book is presented as a moral tale—the journey of a New Age Candide—exploring the dangers of uninvited programming. It even includes lessons on how to counter-program and reprogram destructive programming, be it from a cult leader, a relative, the Tobacco Institute, or yourself. Peter McWilliams explains what we can do to obtain and maintain our personal freedom—a difficult but rewarding task. 424 pages. **Hardcover,** $19.95.

### *Come Love With Me & Be My Life*
#### *The Complete Romantic Poetry of Peter McWilliams*

Touching, direct, emotional, often funny, this is the best of Peter McWilliams's romantic poetry. 250 pages. **Hardcover,** $12.95. **Audio tapes** (unabridged, two cassettes, read by the author), $12.95.

### *I Marry You Because . . .*

Poetry and quotations on love and marriage. 192 pages. **Trade paperback,** $5.95.

### *PORTRAITS: A Book of Photographs*

The first published collection of Peter McWilliams's photographs, focuses on portraits of people. The book is a large format (9x12) and features more than 200 black & white and color photographs, exquisitely printed. 252 pages. **Hardcover,** $34.95.

To order any of these books,
please check your local bookstore, or call

# 1–800–LIFE–101

or write to

**Prelude Press**
8159 Santa Monica Boulevard
Los Angeles, California 90046

**Please write or call for our free catalog!**

# Index

# C

527

## Q

## R